THE GRACE
OF MARY TRAVERSE

By Timberlake Wertenbaker

**DRAMATISTS
PLAY SERVICE
INC.**

THE GRACE OF MARY TRAVERSE was first produced at The Royal Court Theatre on October 17, 1985, with the following cast.

MARY TRAVERSE .... Janet McTeer
GILES TRAVERSE .... Harold Innocent
MRS. TEMPTWELL .... Pam Ferris
LORD GORDON .... Tom Chadbon
AN OLD WOMAN .... Jonathan Phillips
SOPHIE............................... Eve Matheson
MR. MANNERS .... James Smith
THE BOY .... Jonathan Phillips
MR. HARDLONG...................... David Beames
LORD EXRAKE...................... Harold Innocent
ROBERT........................... Jonathan Phillips
JACK .... David Beames
THE GUARD........................ Jonathan Phillips
THE SPY .... James Smith
THE LOCKSMITH .... Tom Chadbon
OLD WOMAN............................ Pam Ferris
OLD WOMAN......................... Eve Matheson
THE MAN .... Tom Chadbon

DIRECTED BY .... Danny Boyle
DESIGNED BY .... Kandis Cook
LIGHTING BY.................... Christopher Toulmin

CHARACTERS

MARY TRAVERSE
GILES TRAVERSE
MRS. TEMPTWELL
LORD GORDON
AN OLD WOMAN
SOPHIE
MR. MANNERS
BOY
MR. HARDLONG
LORD EXRAKE
ROBERT
AN OLD WOMAN
ANOTHER OLD WOMAN
JACK
GUARD
SPY
LOCKSMITH
THE MAN

London, the late 18th Century

For John.

If you are squeamish
Don't prod the beach rubble

Sappho
Translated from the Greek by Mary Barnard
(University of California Press)

It may be that it is a mere fatuity, an indecency to debate of the
definition of culture in the age of the gas-oven, of the arctic camps,
of napalm. The topic may belong solely to the past history of hope.
But we should not take this contingency to be a natural fact of life, a
platitude. We must keep in focus its hideous novelty or renovation
... The numb prodigality of our acquaintance with horror is a radical
human defect.

George Steiner, *In Bluebeard's Castle*
(Faber and Faber)

NOTE:
Although this play is set in the eighteenth century, it is not a historical play. All the characters are my own invention and whenever I
have used historical events such as the Gordon Riots I have taken
great freedom with reported fact. I found the eighteenth century a
valid metaphor, and I was concerned to free the people of the play
from contemporary preconceptions.

The game of piquet in Act II, scene 4, was devised with the help of
David Parlett.

THE GRACE OF MARY TRAVERSE

ACT ONE
Scene 1:

The drawing room of a house in the City of London during the late eighteenth century. Mary Traverse sits elegantly, facing an empty chair. She talks to the chair with animation. Giles Traverse stands behind and away from her.

MARY. Nature, my lord. *(Pause.)* It was here all the time and we've only just discovered it. What is nature? No, that's a direct question. Perhaps we will not exhaust nature as easily as we have other pleasures for it is difficult to imagine with what to replace it. And there's so much of it! No, that's too enthusiastic. *(Short pause.)* How admirable of you to have shown us the way, my lord, to have made the grand tour of such a natural place as Wales. Ah, crags, precipices, what awe they must strike in one's breas— in one's spirit. Yes. And I hear Wales even has peasants. How you must have admired the austerity of their lives, their human nature a complement to the land's starkness. Peasants too I believe are a new discovery. How delightful of our civilisation to shed light on its own dark and savage recesses. Oh dear, is that blue stockinged or merely incomprehensible? When you said the other day that he who is tired of London is tired of life, did you mean — but how foolish of me. It was Doctor Johnson. Forgive the confusion, you see there are so few men of wit about. *(Pause)* You were telling me how we are to know nature. Do we dare look at it directly, or do we trust an artist's imitation, a poet, the paintings of Mr. Gainsborough. Whirlpools. Trees. Primordial matter. Circling. Indeed. Oh. *(Mary stops in a panic. Giles Traverse clears his throat. Mary talks faster.)* You visited the salt mines? Ah, to hover over the depths in a basket and then to plunge deep down into the earth, into its very bowels.

GILES. No, no, my dear, do not mention bowels. Especially after dinner.

MARY. To have no more than a fragile rope between oneself and utter destruction. How thrilling!

GILES. No, Mary. It shakes your frame with terror and you begin to faint.

MARY. I wouldn't faint, Papa. I'd love to visit a salt mine.

GILES. You are here not to express your desires but to make conversation.

MARY. Can desire not be part of a conversation?

GILES. No. To be agreeable, a young woman must make the other person say interesting things.

MARY. He hasn't said a word.

GILES. Ah, but he won't know that. Now faint, and even the most tongue-tied fop will ask how you are. That allows you to catch your breath and begin again.

MARY. How clever of you, Papa. And the rivers...

GILES. There's too much of this nature in your conversation.

MARY. It is what people are thinking about.

GILES. Sounds foreign. I shall bring it up at the next meeting of the antigallican society.

MARY. Oh Papa, I could come and explain—

GILES. You? Now move onto another subject. This is difficult: leave no gap, you must glide into it. Converse, Mary, converse.

MARY. I can't think what follows naturally from nature. Ah: I hear God is ... no ... I believe God—

GILES. Talk of God leads to silence, Mary.

MARY. The architecture of—

GILES. Too athletic. People might think you spend time out of doors.

MARY. Reason, they say ... is that too Popish?

GILES. No, but a woman talking about reason is like a merchant talking about the nobility. It smacks of ambition. I overheard that in a coffee house. Good, isn't it?

MARY. But Papa you're always talking about lords and you're a merchant.

GILES. I am not. Not exactly. Who told you this?

MARY. I look out of the window and see coaches with your name.

GILES. Why gape out of the window when I've given you so much to see in the house? I have land. There are potteries on it, but that's acceptable. Lord Folly has mines on his. And it's not refined to look too closely at the source of one's wealth. Now, you have a methodist preacher here and a rake there. Keep them from the weather.

MARY. Books? Preachers don't read. Music? That's for afternoon tea with the ladies. Drink? No...

GILES. It's obvious. Praise England: patriotism.

MARY. But Papa, you won't let me study politics. And I'd so like to.

GILES. Patriotism is to politics what the fart is to the digestion. Euh, you're not to repeat that, although it was said by a very grand lady. A duchess. Say something against the Americans and fop, fool, rattle, mathematician and gambler will easily add to it.

MARY. Are we at war with them yet? Have you made another brillant speech?

GILES. Yes. I demonstrated logically that God gave us the colonies for the sole purpose of advantageous trade. We are interested in their raw materials but not in their ideas. Ambitious upstarts! We'll finish now, I'm going to the theatre.

MARY. Let me come with you, Papa. It will help my conversation.

GILES. There's no need to see a play to talk about it. I'll bring you the playbill. We'll continue tomorrow with repartee and do a little better, I hope.

MARY. Wouldn't I do better if I saw a little more of the world?

GILES. I'm afraid that's not possible. Don't be sad. You have tried today and I'll reward you with a kiss.

MARY. Thank you, Papa.

GILES. You are my brightest adornment, my dear. I want to be proud of my daughter.

MARY. Yes, Papa.

GILES. You are my joy and my hope.

MARY. But Papa—

GILES. A compliment must be received in silence, Mary. The French always protest at compliments, but that's because they're so tediously argumentative. Goodbye.

MARY. Goodbye, Papa.

Scene 2:

The drawing room. Mary, alone, walks back and forth across a carpet. She stops occasionally and examines the area on which she has just stepped.

MARY. Almost. *(She walks. Stops and examines.)* Yes. Better. *(She walks again. Looks.)* Ah. There. *(She walks faster now, then examines.)* I've done it. See the invisible passage of an amiable woman. *(Pause.)* It was the dolls who gave me my first lessons. No well-made doll, silk-limbed, satin-clothed, leaves an imprint. As a child I lay still and believed their weightlessness mine. Awkward later to discover I grew, weighed. Best not to move very much. But nature was implacable. More flesh, more weight. Embarrassment all around. So the teachers came. Air, they said. Air? Air. I waited, a curious child, delighted by the prospect of knowledge. Air. You must become like air. Weightless. Still. Invisible. Learn to drop a fan and wait. When that is perfected, you may move, slightly, from the waist only. Later, dare to walk, but leave no trace. Now my presence will be as pleasing as my step, leaving no memory. I am complete: unruffled landscape. I may sometimes be a little bored, but my manners are excellent. And if I think too much, my feet no longer betray this. *(She walks.)* What comes after, what is even more graceful than air? *(She tries to tiptoe, then stamps the ground and throws down her fan.)* Damn! *(She stands still and holds her breath.)*

Mrs. Temptwell! *(Mrs. Temptwell comes on immediately. Short silence.)* My fan.

MRS. TEMPTWELL. It's broken.

MARY. I dropped it.

MRS. TEMPTWELL. A bad fall, Miss Mary.

MARY. Pick it up, please. *(Mrs. Temptwell does so, with bad grace.)*

MRS. TEMPTWELL. I have work to do.

MARY. Bring me some hot milk.

MRS. TEMPTWELL. I'll call the chambermaid.

MARY. Watch me, Mrs. Temptwell. Do I look ethereal?

MRS. TEMPTWELL. You do look a little ill, Miss Mary, yes.

MARY. You don't understand anything. I'm trying not to breathe.

MRS. TEMPTWELL. Your mother was good at that.

MARY. Was she?

MRS. TEMPTWELL. Said it thickened the waist. She died of not breathing in the end, poor thing, may she rest in peace, I'm sure she does, she always did.

MARY. Could she walk on a carpet and leave no imprint?

MRS. TEMPTWELL. She went in and out of rooms with no one knowing she'd been there. She was so quiet, your mother, it took the master a week to notice she was dead. But she looked ever so beautiful in her coffin and he couldn't stop looking at her. Death suits women. You'd look lovely in a coffin, Miss Mary.

MARY. I don't need a coffin to look lovely, Mrs. Temptwell.

MRS. TEMPTWELL. No, some women don't even have to die, they look dead already, but that doesn't work as well. It's better to be dead and look as if you'd been alive than the other way, if you get my meaning, as if you'd been dead all the time, quiet and dull.

MARY. I don't look like that.

MRS. TEMPTWELL. Only when you've been reading.

MARY. Oh. Some books are dull. *The Young Ladies Conduct. Caesar's Wars.*

MRS. TEMPTWELL. It's a strange thing about books, they

11

make the face go funny. I had an uncle who took to books. He went all gray. Then he went mad. May I go now?

MARY. Your uncle doesn't count. Books improve the mind. Am I not charming and witty? *(Silence.)* That girl in number fourteen, the one you keep telling me about, she must read.

MRS. TEMPTWELL. Oh no, she's too busy sitting at her window, staring at everything.

MARY. Gaping? She must have nothing to look at in her own house, poor thing.

MRS. TEMPTWELL. She even asked one of the servents to take her out on the street.

MARY. Outside? On foot? She did? Oh. But her reputation?

MRS. TEMPTWELL. Disguised. No one will know. I wish you could see her, Miss Mary, she...

MARY. What?

MRS. TEMPTWELL. Glitters with interest.

MARY. Glitters? How vulgar. Where's my milk?

MRS. TEMPTWELL. Your mother wanted to go out once in her life, but she died before we could manage it. I felt sorry she missed that one little pleasure.

MARY. Papa wouldn't have been pleased.

MRS. TEMPTWELL. The master doesn't see everything. I'll fetch your milk now.

MARY. What's so different out there? When I ride in my carriage I see nothing of interest.

MRS. TEMPTWELL. That's because the streets have to be emptied to make way for your carriage. It's different on foot. Very different. Would you prefer a glass of ratafia?

MARY. Wait.

MRS. TEMPTWELL. I haven't got all day.

MARY. What harm could once do? It'll only improve my conversation and Papa will admire me. Yes, Mrs. Temptwell, you'll take me.

MRS. TEMPTWELL. Take you where, Miss Mary?

MARY. You know very well. You'll take me out there. Yes. Into the streets. I'll glitter with knowledge.

MRS. TEMPTWELL. I can't do that, I'll lose my place.
MARY. We'll go disguised, as you suggested.
MRS. TEMPTWELL. I didn't, Miss Mary, I never did.
MARY. I've decided, Mrs. Temptwell, we're going out.
MRS. TEMPTWELL. What have I done?
MARY. I'll pay you.
MRS. TEMPTWELL. You always make me talk too much.

Scene 3:

Cheapside, London. Lord Gordon comes on.

LORD GORDON. My name is George Gordon. Lord Gordon. *(Pause.)* Nothing. No reaction. No one's interested. *(Pause.)* It's always like this. I greet people, their eyes glaze. I ride in Hyde Park, my horse falls asleep. *(Pause.)* I am a man of stunning mediocrity. *(Pause.)* This can't go on. I must do something. Now. But what? How does Mr. Manners make everyone turn around? Of course: politics. I'll make a speech in the House: all criminals must be severely punished. But stealing a handkerchief is already a hanging matter. I know: make England thrifty, enclose the common land. I think that's been done. Starve the poor to death! Perhaps politics is too ambitious. I'll write. Even women do that now. But about what? No, I'll be a wit. I'll make everyone laugh at what I say. But I'll have to think of something funny. Sir John's a rake, that's a possibility. But the ladies are so demanding and my manhood won't rise above middling. Shall I die in a duel? No. This is desperate. Perhaps I'm seen with the wrong people. They're all so brilliant. In a different world, I might shine. Here are some ordinary people. They must notice me, if only because I'm a lord. Oh God, please make me be noticed, just once. Please show me the way. *(Lord Gordon adopts an interesting pose. An Old Woman walks on, very slowly.)* Hm. *(She looks at him and continues walking. Sophie comes on.)*

SOPHIE. Please— *(The Old Woman turns around.)* No, you're not...I'm sorry. I'm looking for someone called Polly. *(Pause.)* My aunt...I'm to find her here. This is Cheapside? *(The Old Woman nods.)* She has her pitch here. I've come to work for her. You don't know where she is? *(The Old Woman shakes her head.)* I'm not sure what she looks like. I haven't seen her for such a long time. *(Pause.)* Where could she be? *(The Old Woman shrugs.)* I don't know anyone. *(The Old Woman walks away.)* What am I going to do? *(The Old Woman moves off.)* London's so big.

LORD GORDON. Hhm. *(Sophie looks briefly at him and goes off.)*

SOPHIE. I must find Aunt Polly. *(Mary and Mrs. Temptwell come on.)*

MARY. I believe I've just stepped on something unpleasant, Mrs. Temptwell. These streets are filthy.

MRS. TEMPTWELL. The dirt runs out of great houses like yours.

MARY. What? I don't like this world. It's nasty.

MRS. TEMPTWELL. If you're squeamish, don't stir the beach rubble.

MARY. What did you say?

MRS. TEMPTWELL. It's a saying we had in our family.

MARY. Did you have a family? I can't imagine you anywhere but in our house.

MRS. TEMPTWELL. Lack of imagination has always been a convenience of the rich.

LORD GORDON. HHmm.

MARY. What? I do wish these people weren't so ugly. *(The Old Woman comes on.)*

MRS. TEMPTWELL. Their life is hard.

MARY. They ought to go back to the country and be beautiful peasants.

MRS. TEMPTWELL. They've already been thrown off the land. Some of them were farmers.

MARY. Papa says farmers stop progress. I meant beautiful peasants I could talk about with grace. There's nothing here to

14

improve my conversation.

MRS. TEMPTWELL. It takes time to turn misery into an object of fun.

LORD GORDON. *(Louder.)* HHmmm.

MARY. Why does that man keep clearing his throat?

MRS. TEMPTWELL. I don't know. He doesn't look mad.

MARY. I want to go back.

MRS. TEMPTWELL. So soon, Miss Mary? Such a dull appetite?

MARY. I might be curious about the plague and not care to embrace the dead bodies. This ugliness looks contagious. I'm going.

LORD GORDON. No. This is intolerable. You can't go without noticing me. My name is George Gordon. Lord Gordon.

MARY. Let's go.

LORD GORDON. How dare someone like you ignore me. You!

MARY. Mrs. Temptwell, I'm frightened.

LORD GORDON. I don't want you to be frightened. Wait. Yes. Are you very frightened?

MARY. No, not very.

LORD GORDON. How dare you! *(He takes out his sword.)* Now. Now you're very frightened. I can see it. Why didn't I think of this before?

MARY. I want to go home.

LORD GORDON. Not yet. I'll make you even more frightened. Yes. I'll show you my strength. Come over here to the lampost.

MARY. Help! Mrs. Temptwell!

MRS. TEMPTWELL. This is the world. *(Sophie comes on.)*

SOPHIE. Please—

MRS. TEMPTWELL. Damn!

SOPHIE. Oh. I'm sorry...Have you by any chance seen my aunt? Her name's Polly...what's there?

MRS. TEMPTWELL. Nothing for you, girl. Go away. Quickly.

SOPHIE. But he's—

MRS. TEMPTWELL. So what? It could be you. *(Sophie goes*

15

towards Lord Gordon and Mary.)

SOPHIE. Leave her alone, Sir. What are you doing?

LORD GORDON. Everyone pays me attention now. Who are you? I'll have you too.

SOPHIE. No, Sir, please Sir. Please— *(Lord Gordon grabs Sophie. Mary gets away.)*

LORD GORDON. Beg. Yes. Beg for mercy. Beg.

SOPHIE. Please have mercy, Sir.

LORD GORDON. What delight! Say over and over again Lord Gordon have mercy on me. Say it.

SOPHIE. Lord Gordon have mercy on me.

LORD GORDON. Again, again. On your knees and keep saying my name.

SOPHIE. Lord Gordon have mercy on me. Lord Gordon. Lord Gordon.

LORD GORDON. My strength rises. I can't contain myself. Over here.

MARY. Call for help, Mrs. Temptwell.

MRS. TEMPTWELL. Why?

MARY. What will he do to her?

MRS. TEMPTWELL. Rape her. But she won't mind. Virtue, like ancestors, is a luxury of the rich. Watch and you'll learn something.

MARY. Rape? What the Greek gods did? Will he turn himself into a swan, a bull, a shower of golden rain? Is he a God?

MRS. TEMPTWELL. He'll feel like one.

MARY. He stands her against the lampost, sword gleaming at her neck, she's quiet. Now the sword lifts up her skirts, no words between them, the sword is his voice and his will. He thrusts himself against her, sword in the air. He goes on and on. She has no expression on her face. He shudders. She's still. He turns away from her, tucks the sword away. I couldn't stop looking. *(Pause.)* It's not like the books. *(Mr. Manners comes on.)* Sir, be careful, there's someone—

MR. MANNERS. Go away, I only give money to organized charities. Lord Gordon. I was looking for you.

16

LORD GORDON. Mr. Manners. I was just thinking of you.

MR. MANNERS. Have I disturbed you?

LORD GORDON. Not at all. I'm finished.

MR. MANNERS. Who are these women?

LORD GORDON. Just women. What shall we do tonight? I feel exceptionally lively.

MR. MANNERS. We might play a game of piquet.

LORD GORDON. Yes. I'll win. My fortune has turned.

MR. MANNERS. Delighted. Shall we have supper before?

LORD GORDON. I've never felt so hungry. Let's eat at a chop house.

MR. MANNERS. There's something on at the Opera.

LORD GORDON. But first, let's go to a Coffee House. I have some witticisms.

MR. MANNERS. You, Lord Gordon?

LORD GORDON. Mr. Manners, I'm a different man

MR. MANNERS. What's happened? A legacy?

LORD GORDON. *(Quietly.)* Power.

MR. MANNERS. Ah. Power.

LORD GORDON. Isn't power something you know all about?

MR. MANNERS. Yes, but it is not something I ever discuss.

(They go. Sophie comes down towards Mary, walking with pain. They look at each other. Then Sophie moves off.)

MARY. *(Looking at the ground.)* Blood.

Scene 4:

Outside the Universal Coffee House in Fleet Street. Boy, an eighteenth century waiter, blocks Mary and Mrs. Temptwell.

BOY. You can't.

MARY. They've just gone in.

BOY. You can't come in.

MARY. We're following them.

BOY. Ladies wait outside.

MRS. TEMPTWELL. Ask him why?

BOY. They don't like to be disturbed.

MARY. I know how to talk.

BOY. They don't do ladies talk.

MARY. What sex is wit?

MRS. TEMPTWELL. Ask him who's in there.

BOY. Mr. Fielding, Mr. Goldsmith, Mr. Hume, Mr. Boswell, Mr. Garrick, the Doctor, Mr. Sheridan, Mr. Hogarth.

MARY. But I know them all very well. I've often imagined talking to them. Let me in immediately.

BOY. And some foreigners. Mr. Piranesis, Mr. Tyepolo, Mr. Hayden, Mr. Voltairt, Mr. Leibniz, Mr. Wolgang. They're quiet the foreigners, and no one listens to them. You have to stay out. Orders.

MRS. TEMPTWELL. Ask him why they let him in.

BOY. I'm the boy. I go everywhere.

MARY. I don't understand.

BOY. I'll let you see through the window.

MARY. I've spent my life looking through window panes. I want to face them.

BOY. Wouldn't be right.

MRS. TEMPTWELL. Doesn't right belong to those who take it?

BOY. I don't ask questions.

MRS. TEMPTWELL. Don't you wish you could be like him?

MARY. Yes. No. Envy is a sin, Mrs. Temptwell.

MRS. TEMPTWELL. And heaven must be a lady's tea party: the jingling of beatific stupidity.

MARY. What's happened to me? I was happy in my rooms.

MRS. TEMPTWELL. Think of what you've seen.

MARY. I've seen them walk the streets without fear, stuff food into their mouths with no concern for their waists. I've seen them tear into skin without hesitation and litter the streets with their dis-

18

carded actions. But I have no map to this world. I walk it as a foreigner and sense only danger.

BOY. I never stay anywhere long. There's too much to do.

MARY. Be quiet!

BOY. It's a waste of time being kind to women.

MARY. I'm going to hate you. No, that's an ugly feeling.

MRS. TEMPTWELL. Why waste your time hating him, Mary? You could be like him if you wanted to. But there's a price.

BOY. Her soul.

MRS. TEMPTWELL. We're not so medieval, Boy. We're protestants and the century's enlightened. *(To Mary.)* Do you want to travel in their world? Around every corner, the glitter of a possibility. You'll no longer be an ornate platter served for their tasting. No, you'll feast with them. No part of flesh or mind unexplored. No horizon ever fixed. Experience! *(Pause.)* I could manage it for you.

BOY. We're not deceived when they dress as men. A lady came to us masqueraded. We uncovered her. All of her.

MRS. TEMPTWELL. Do I sound so superficial? Well, Mary?

MARY. Run the world through my fingers as they do. *(Pause.)* Oh yes, I want it. Yes. What's the price?

MRS. TEMPTWELL. You'll stay with me.

MARY. Yes, but the price?

MRS. TEMPTWELL. You can never go back. *(Pause.)* Have they ever asked to live like us?

MARY. No, they're too busy. But I want the world as it is, Mrs. Temptwell, no imitations, no illusions, I want to know it all.

MRS. TEMPTWELL. You'll know all you want to know.

BOY. Will you sign a contract?

MRS. TEMPTWELL. It's done. You can go back inside, boy.

BOY. It's more interesting out here this evening. May I stay?

MRS. TEMPTWELL. See now, Mary who's outside.

MARY. Yes. Yes. How will I pay you, Mrs. Temptwell?

MRS. TEMPTWELL. Don't worry. You'll pay.

ACT TWO
Scene 1:

The Brothers Club. Giles Traverse, Mr. Manners.

MR. MANNERS. Three days?

GILES. Three.

MR. MANNERS. And the letter?

GILES. Only that her dear Papa would understand, she'd gone to investigate the very underside of nature. I thought she meant Vauxhall Gardens. I don't approve of course, but Lord Oldland told me his daughter often went to Vauxhall, masked, and never came to any harm.

MR. MANNERS. Have you told anyone?

GILES. No. I went to Bow-Street.

MR. MANNERS. My dear Giles, you might as well have gone straight to the papers.

GILES. It is my daughter, Manners. She could have been kidnapped.

MR. MANNERS. This isn't France. You said she left with a servant. An elopement?

GILES. No. Manners, you must know someone who can investigate, discreetly.

MR. MANNERS. No one in politics can afford the cost of a secret, Giles, not even you. No. There's nothing you can do. Forget her.

GILES. Forget my daughter!

MR. MANNERS. Do you think most of the men in this club know where their children are? Or who they are, for that matter.

GILES. I have only one daughter.

MR. MANNERS. You have only one country. The King, Giles, wants new men in the Cabinet. Men of intelligence and ambition, who show strength of character. There has been mention of you. But should there be a scandal...

GILES. The Cabinet. Now?

MR. MANNERS. These are difficult times. I had the impression you had a strong sense of duty. Perhaps I was wrong...

GILES. After all these years. Why now?

MR. MANNERS. You of all people should know: supply and demand. People have become suspicious of the old families. But the old families do know how to conduct themselves... *(Lord Gordon comes on.)*

LORD GORDON. Giles. Just the man I was looking for.

GILES. My lord.

LORD GORDON. I have made a momentous decision. Yes. I've decided to get married. It's what I need: a wife to look up to me. I have decided to marry your daughter.

GILES. You've seen her!

LORD GORDON. How could I? You've never presented her. I don't want to marry a woman I know. You've said your daughter is pretty and clever. She's not too clever, is she? She won't talk at breakfast? I couldn't bear that. *(Silence.)* She hasn't married someone else, has she? I'll kill him in a duel. I wouldn't mind marrying a widow: less to explain.

MR. MANNERS. Giles's daughter died yesterday, of a bad chill.

GILES. Mr. Manners!

MR. MANNERS. I know how painful it is for you, Giles. We won't mention her again.

LORD GORDON. How inconvenient. I'll have to think of something else. You don't have any other daughters, do you?

GILES. No. Mr. Manners, I—

MR. MANNERS. At least she went quietly, Giles, we must be thankful for that. I'll speak to the King, he may find a way to ease your grief. Kings have such curative powers.

LORD GORDON. I think I'll be brokenhearted over your daughter's death, Giles, it'll make me interesting.

Scene 2 :

The study of Giles Traverse. He is in some disarray. Mrs. Temptwell is dressed for the street.

GILES. Where is she?

MRS. TEMPTWELL. Don't you know? You buried her.

GILES. Who are you?

MRS. TEMPTWELL. I've been in your house for twenty-five years, Sir.

GILES. I know that, Mrs. Temptwell. Why have you done this?

MRS. TEMPTWELL. Done what, Sir? I've always done what Mary asked. She used to want cups of tea. Now she wants other things.

GILES. I'll have you thrown in prison.

MRS. TEMPTWELL. For what? Killing her? I might have to tell people she's still alive. Think of the questions...

GILES. I trusted you with the care of my daughter. Was Mary not kind to you?

MRS. TEMPTWELL. As she might be to the chair she sat on. She cared for my use.

GILES. What more can a servant expect?

MRS. TEMPTWELL. Do you remember my father? He was a farmer when you were a farmer. His land was next to yours.

GILES. I must have bought it.

MRS. TEMPTWELL. He trusted you to leave him his cottage. When you landscaped your garden, you needed a lake. The cottage was drowned in the lake.

GILES. I gave those people work.

MRS. TEMPTWELL. He went to one of your potteries. He died.

GILES. And it's because of your father's misfortune that you've killed my daughter?

MRS. TEMPTWELL. Your daughter's only dead for you. That's your misfortune.

22

GILES. Please tell me where she is.

MRS. TEMPTWELL. She's not ready to see you. She hasn't yet learned to be a ghost.

GILES. I'll give you anything you want.

MRS. TEMPTWELL. You've already done that.

GILES. I don't understand.

MRS. TEMPTWELL. It's simple, Giles Traverse. When a man cries, he could be anybody.

Scene 3:

Lodgings in Marylebone. Mrs. Temptwell stands in the background and watches. Mary is fully dressed. Mr. Hardlong is naked. They remain far apart.

MR. HARDLONG. You ask for pleasure. Why do you cringe as if expecting violence? *(Short silence.)* If you believe violence will bring you pleasure, you've been misled. The enjoyment of perversion is not a physical act but a metaphysical one. You want pleasure: come and take it. *(Silence. Mary does not move.)* Are you pretending you've never felt desire unfurl in your blood? Never known the gnawing of flesh, that gaping hunger of the body? Never sensed the warm dribble of your longings? Come, come, need isn't dainty and it's no good calling cowardice virginity. *(Mary squirms a little.)* Perhaps you want me to seduce you and let you remain irresponsible? I promised you physical pleasure, not the tickle of self reproach and repentance, the squirm of the soul touching itself in its intimate parts. Or are you waiting for a declaration of love? Let romance blunt the sting of your need, mask a selfish act with selfless acquiescence? Novels, my dear, novels. And in the end, your body remains dry. What are you waiting for? Pleasure requires activity. Come. *(Mary moves a little closer and closes her eyes.)* Ah, yes. Close the eyes, let the act remain dark. Cling to your ignorance,

23

the mind's last chastity. A man's body is beautiful, Mary, and ought to be known. I'll even give you some advice, for free: never take a man you don't find beautiful. If you have to close your eyes when he comes near you, turn away, walk out of the room and never look back. You may like his words, his promises, his wit, his soul, but wrapping your legs around a man's talent will bring no fulfillment. No, open your eyes. Look at me. *(Mary looks, unfocused.)* The neck is beautiful, Mary, but doesn't require endless study. Look down. The arms have their appeal and the hands hold promise. The chest can be charming, the ribs melancholic. Look down still. They call these the loins, artists draw their vulnerability, but you're not painting a martyrdom. Look now. *(Mary focuses on his penis.)* See how delicate the skin, how sweetly it blushes at your look. It will start at your touch, obey your least guidance. It's one purpose to serve you and you'd make it an object of fear? Look, Mary, shaped for your delight, intricacies for your play, here is the wand of your pleasure, nature's generous magic. I'm here for you. Act now. You have hands, use them. Take what you want, Mary. Take it. *(Mary stretches out her hand.)*

MARY. At first, power. I am the flesh's alchemist. Texture hardens at my touch, subterranean rivers follow my fingers. I pull back the topsoil, skim the nakedness of matter. All grows in my hand. Now to my needs. Ouch! No one warned me about the pain, not so pleasant that. Scratch the buttocks in retaliation, convenient handles and at my mercy. And now to the new world. Ah, but this is much better than climbing mountains in Wales. I plunge to the peaks again and again with the slightest adjustment. One, two, three, change of angle, change of feel. This is delightful and I'm hardly breathless. Again. Not Welsh this, the Alps at least: exploding sunshine, waterfalls, why is this geography not in the books? On to the rolling waves of the Bay of Biscay, I would go on forever, why have you stopped, Mr. Hardlong, have you crashed on the cape? You don't answer, Mr. Hardlong, you're pale and short of breath. I am the owner of this mine and there are seams still untouched. You mustn't withdraw your labour. You seem a little dead, Mr. Hardlong. I want more.

24

MRS. TEMPTWELL. We'll have to find you someone else, Mary.

MARY. I like this one. I love you, Mr. Hardlong, yes, I do. I thought I loved my father, but that was cold. This is hot. Don't turn away, Mr. Hardlong, please don't die.

MRS. TEMPTWELL. Don't be sentimental, labour's expendable.

MARY. He's reviving! Oh, joy!

MR. HARDLONG. Where's my gold?

MARY. Here, Mr. Hardlong, take it. And bring food to revive us, Mrs. Temptwell. A duck, some good roast beef, and a pudding of bread and butter, very sweet. You'll eat with me, Mr. Hardlong.

MR. HARDLONG. I don't have time. Where is she?

MARY. Who?

MR. HARDLONG. You promised she'd be here, Mrs. Temptwell.

MRS. TEMPTWELL. I haven't forgotten. *(She calls.)* Sophie! *(Sophie comes on, bringing food. Mary pounces on it.)*

MARY. *(Eating.)* I've seen you before. I remember now: Lord Gordon. I was sorry.

MRS. TEMPTWELL. *(Touching Sophie's stomach.)* Observe how mediocrity loves to duplicate itself. Take the rest of your payment, Mr. Hardlong.

MR. HARDLONG. *(To Sophie.)* Come with me.

SOPHIE. Mrs. Temptwell, you didn't tell me—

MRS. TEMPTWELL. Do you want to starve on the streets?

MR. HARDLONG. Don't be afraid, I won't hurt you.

SOPHIE. You said I was to work for a lady.

MRS. TEMPTWELL. So you are. Mr. Hardlong's price was high. You're saving Mary half her gold. That's what servants are for.

MR. HARDLONG. Come quickly.

MARY. Mr. Hardlong.

MR. HARDLONG. Look. I have gold.

MARY. Mr. Hardlong, please.

MR. HARDLONG. What is it, Mary. You see I'm in a hurry.

MARY. At least answer one question. I paid you a good sum for what we did.

MR. HARDLONG. Fifty guineas.

MARY. You'll give it to Sophie?

MR. HARDLONG. All of it.

MARY. For the same thing we did?

MR. HARDLONG. The same.

MARY. I pay you. You pay her. I don't understand.

MR. HARDLONG. I gave you pleasure, Mary.

MARY. Yes. You did. Yes.

MR. HARDLONG. Did you offer me any?

MARY. I confess I forgot a little about you. But weren't we doing the same thing?

MR. HARDLONG. I had to look after your well-being.

MARY. You mean we were at the same table but I let you beg while I feasted? I see. But Sophie?

MR. HARDLONG. Will serve my luxury.

MARY. I would do that too, Mr. Hardlong. I would advocate the community of pleasure. Teach me what to do and I will.

MR. HARDLONG. It's too late, Mary: you would have to learn to ask for nothing. *(Mr. Hardlong and Sophie go. Mary eats pensively, but nonetheless grossly.)*

MARY. Which do I like best? The first taste on the palate or the roast skin crinkling on the tongue? I like to swallow too. I'm still hungry. *(She stops.)* It's not really hunger, it's a void in the pit of my stomach. Knowledge scoops out its own walls and melancholy threatens. Yes, but I didn't have to leave my rooms to learn that nature abhors a void. What comes next, Mrs. Temptwell, what comes next?

Scene 4:

A large den in Drury Lane. Lord Exrake and Mr. Manners are playing piquet. Young Robert is watching sulkily. Mary, Sophie and Mrs. Temptwell come on.

MR. MANNERS. Carte Blanche. *(Lord Exrake discards five cards.)*

MARY. Cards, numbers, chance, mystery and gain. Oh what a rich and generous world.

MRS. TEMPTWELL. For some.

MARY. Don't be glum, Mrs. Temptwell, let me enjoy it all.

LORD EXRAKE. Six and a seizième.

MARY. And look over there, a cock fight. Shall we go there or play cards? What do you want to do, Sophie?

SOPHIE. Me?...I don't know...

MRS. TEMPTWELL. Our Sophie has no desires.

SOPHIE. Please...

ROBERT. *(Moving towards Sophie.)* What's your name?

MARY. But causes desires in others. I don't understand the world yet, but I will, I will.

MR. MANNERS. You're over the hundred, Lord Exrake.

LORD EXRAKE. Am I, dear boy? So I am, so I am. Robert, why aren't you watching this?

ROBERT. I don't want to learn piquet, Uncle. I think cards are stupid.

LORD EXRAKE. What have you been doing at Oxford all this time?

ROBERT. Studying.

LORD EXRAKE. Whoever heard of studying at Oxford? Meet people, boy, meet people. Another deal, Mr. Manners?

MARY. You play, Sophie, I'll go and watch the fight.

SOPHIE. I can't.

MARY. I'll give you the money and you can keep what you win.

SOPHIE. No...

MARY. Try a little pleasure, Sophie, do. Let's play cards.

MRS. TEMPTWELL. Be careful.

MARY. Why?

ROBERT. *(To Sophie.)* When I inherit his money, I'm going to build a school for women.

SOPHIE. Oh.

27

ROBERT. It will help all these lost girls find virtue and religion again. It's terrible what's happening to women now. I've written a play about it, but no one will put it on. There's a cabal against me and Garrick's a coward.

MR. MANNERS. Piqued, repiqued and capoted. You have all the luck tonight, Lord Exrake.

LORD EXRAKE. At my age, dear boy, there is no luck, only science. *(He sees the women.)* Ah, look, beauties are approaching us. We are having a visitation, a visitation from the fair sex. Let us hail them. *(Lord Exrake messes up the cards.)* You owe me four hundred fifty pounds.

MR. MANNERS. Another deal, Lord Exrake, so I can win back some of my losses.

LORD EXRAKE. No, no, dear boy, don't win, don't win. Qui perd au jeu gagne á l'amour, and of course, vice versa. Do they still teach you young boys French? Ah, l'amour, l'amour, what good is gold without l'amour. Is that not so, mesdemoiselles?

MARY. No, my lord, for what love must not eventually be paid for? I'll play with you.

LORD EXRAKE. Will you, my dear? There is not so much as there once was, but come and sit on my lap.

MARY. I meant piquet, my lord. I'll sit opposite your lap.

MR. MANNERS. He's not playing anymore.

LORD EXRAKE. Oh, but I didn't say...Mr. Manners, one does not refuse a lady...Remember that, Robert.

ROBERT. *(To Sophie.)* Dirty old man, I can't stand him.

MR. MANNERS. The gambling is serious here.

MARY. Is money ever frivolous, Mr. Manners?

MR. MANNERS. The stakes are high.

MARY. I can pay. Show them our money, Mrs. Temptwell.

MRS. TEMPTWELL. No, no, that's not necessary.

LORD EXRAKE. Indeed, Mademoiselle, a beautiful young lady can always pay, one way or another, we shall come to an amicable arrangement.

MARY. I do not need to sell my flesh, my lord, and yours might not fetch enough. You may chose the stakes.

LORD EXRAKE. You are blunt, mademoiselle, you remind me...

ROBERT. A young woman shouldn't talk like that, it's disgusting. Of course I blame him.

LORD EXRAKE. Ten shillings a point?

MRS. TEMPTWELL. That's too high, Mary.

MARY. Shall we double it?

MR. MANNERS. A pound a point. Don't play, Lord Exrake.

MARY. Are you his keeper?

MR. MANNERS. I believe in keeping a sense of decency in these proceedings.

MARY. Is risk an indecency, Mr. Manners? Shall we make it five pounds a point?

MRS. TEMPTWELL. Five pounds!

LORD EXRAKE. Five pounds then.

ROBERT. That's sinful. It's my inheritance.

LORD EXRAKE. What is your name?

MARY. Mary.

MR. MANNERS. Your other name?

MARY. Do you mean my patronymic? I have none. I'm unfathered.

LORD EXRAKE. *(To Sophie.)* And you, my pretty? Forgive me for not noticing you before, mademoiselle. You're not as tall as your friend, but not so fierce neither. I think I like you better.

MARY. Her name's Sophie. Let's play.

LORD EXRAKE. Sophie...such a beautiful name...You remind me...

ROBERT. *(To Sophie.)* I've never been with a woman— *(Lord Exrake and Mary cut the cards.)*

MARY. I am elder.

LORD EXRAKE. And I the youth. Ah, youth. It was as a mere youth...have I told you, Mr. Manners?

MR. MANNERS. Yes, you have. *(Lord Exrake deals. Mary exchanges five cards. Lord Exrake three.)*

ROBERT. But I know how to write about women. I know what women need. I don't understand why they won't listen.

LORD EXRAKE. It was the nights...The nights aren't the same these days. What do you do with your nights, Mr. Manners?

MR. MANNERS. I spend most of them in the Cabinet trying to quiet the Americans. It's a most trying country.

LORD EXRAKE. We didn't have Americans in my day. The Scots were exotic enough for us. Ah, the old world...Perhaps that's what's wrong with Robert.

MARY. Point of five.

LORD EXRAKE. Making?

MARY. Forty nine.

LORD EXRAKE. Good.

MARY. In hearts. Lord Exrake, it is my hand that should interest you, not my legs. Keep your feet to yourself.

LORD EXRAKE. Alas, don't hobble me, mademoiselle. It was thinking of my youth...Where is the other one, the beautiful Sophie? Come and sit on my lap, my dear, your friend is too severe. That is, if your dear Mama will allow.

MARY. She's not our Mama, she's our duenna. Keeps the grim suitor prudence from our hearts.

MRS. TEMPTWELL. Do what you want with her, Lord Exrake, she never resists.

SOPHIE. Mrs. Temptwell, please—

ROBERT. *(To Sophie.)* When I have my school, you'll be saved from all this. Your work will be hard but decent and you'll celebrate your chastity.

MR. MANNERS. *(To Mary.)* You ought not to be here, Mary. I know who you are.

MARY. How can you when I do not even know myself? Do you know yourself, Mr. Manners?

MRS. TEMPTWELL. Concentrate on the game, Mary.

MARY. And a quart major.

LORD EXRAKE. Good. *(He pulls Sophie to him.)* Do sit on my lap, belle Sophie, your friend frightens me.

MARY. You stand behind me, Mr. Manners, shall I invite you on my lap?

MR. MANNERS. I want to watch you play.

MARY. A voyeur. And I took you for a man of action. That's five for point, four for the sequence: nine.

LORD EXRAKE. No, no, do not try to escape, Sophie.

MARY. Three knaves?

LORD EXRAKE. Three knaves are not good.

MARY. Your suspicions runs down my neck, Mr. Manners, you do not trust the fairness of the fair sex. I promise I've encountered fortune head on, no female detours for me. And one for leading, ten. *(Mary leads to the first trick.)*

LORD EXRAKE. I count fourteen tens and three queens. You talk too much. It is not that I mind women who talk. In the salons, women used to talk, but in the salons, they talked in French...Do you know the salons, Mr. Manners? *(They play their tricks.)*

MR. MANNERS. No. Your discards were good, Mary.

MARY. One learns. To discard. Yours too must be good.

MR. MANNERS. It is more in man's nature.

MARY. Then nature is simply a matter of practice. Eleven, twelve, thirteen, fourteen, fifteen.

LORD EXRAKE. Ah, the salons...Mademoiselle de Lespinasse. I'll give you an introduction, Robert, although now...she spoke to me in the strictest confidence...I was much in demand then. Nineteen, twenty, twenty one, twenty two, twenty three.

MARY. Seventeen, eighteen, and ten for cards, twenty eight. I've won.

MR. MANNERS. Well played. Your hand was weak.

MARY. Did you take me for a fool?

MR. MANNERS. I don't make quick judgements.

MARY. Then you lack imagination. Second deal. *(Mary deals.)*

MR. MANNERS. No. Imagination has been one of my wisest discards.

MARY. You are the elder, Lord Exrake.

LORD EXRAKE. Alas, I am, I am, but once...l'Anglais gallant, they used to call me. Some wag said an Anglais gallant was a contradiction in terms, but Mademoiselle de Lespinasse...Les Anglais, she said, ah, les Anglais. Such phlegmatic exteriors, but beneath tout cela. Quel fire, she said, what feu. Les Anglais...*(Lord Exrake has discarded hesitantly and picked up his new cards.)* Point of seven.

MARY. Not good.

LORD EXRAKE. I have met Italians, she said, no more than gesture deep. Quart minor.

MARY. Not good.

LORD EXRAKE. And the Spanish, who like scorpions sting themselvs to death with their own passion. A trio of Kings.

MARY. Not good.

LORD EXRAKE. Ah. Mm. And the Dutch...The Dutch. One for the heart, makes eight.

MARY. *(Triumphantly.)* Seixiéme for sixteen, a quatorze of knaves, a trio of Aces, that's thirty-three and the repique, ninety-three.

LORD EXRAKE. She had travelled. Will you travel with me, Sophie? Your friend plays too well. *(They play out their tricks. Lord Exrake wins one trick, Mary the rest.)*

MARY. That is yours.

LORD EXRAKE. It was on my travels I met mademoiselle Sophie, or was it Sylvie? She was with that writer, what was his name. Double Entendre, I think. But he wrote so much, and pleasure needs time. It is a demanding vocation. A l'amour comme á la guerre, love and war, the same, ainsi de suite.

MARY. No. A soldier braves death but obeys authority. The pleasure seeker braves authority but gives in to annihilation. This makes pleasure the heroism of the disobedient, whereas war is for those who dare not step out of line, or cowards. An interesting paradox, is it not, Mr. Manners?

MR. MANNERS. I don't like paradoxes, they give me bad dreams.

MARY. I score one hundred and fourteen.

MRS. TEMPTWELL. Stop now, Mary.

MARY. Another game, Lord Exrake?

LORD EXRAKE. I too was bold when I was young. I believed I had time to waste. *(They now play very fast.)*

MARY. I don't waste time, I love it.

LORD EXRAKE. But it isn't wasted time that's so painful, no, wasted time is time that never existed. It's the memories.

MARY. Memories are for the idle, I'll never be idle.

LORD EXRAKE. Memories...those leeches of the mind, exquisite moments, forever past, that now suck you dry.

MARY. I shall never have memories, I won't have time.

MR. MANNERS. Everyone has memories, but they can be changed. An entire people's memory may be changed.

MRS. TEMPTWELL. I live on my memories.

SOPHIE. I like mine.

ROBERT. Mine are awful. My mother was always writing pamphlets. But sometimes the present is worse. *(He goes.)*

LORD EXRAKE. I suffer the torment of Tantalus. I want to reach out my hand to seize those moments and live them again. Do you understand me?

MARY. I score one hundred and twenty.

LORD EXRAKE. It isn't the fear of death that keeps me here all night.

MARY. I sleep as little as I can, the world gives me such pleasure.

LORD EXRAKE. Keeps me here all night, pawing at youth, it's the fear of those memories. The moments mock me with their vanished existence. You'll see.

MARY. Why are you trying to frighten me?

LORD EXRAKE. Why shouldn't you know that age is horrible?

MARY. One hundred and seventy-two. I've lost count of the total.

MRS. TEMPTWELL. Lord Exrake owes you two thousand six hundred and eighty pounds.

MARY. Another game?

LORD EXRAKE. No, no. You remind me of my youth.

MARY. But you have failed to remind me of my old age. Come, Sophie, look at all this delightful money. I could double it before dawn. *(Lord Gordon comes on.)*

LORD EXRAKE. It was the first time I slept through the dawn that the memories took over. There were suddenly too many years between me and the new day. Do I make myself clear? They buzz in my ears and I can't hear. *(Mary turns away.)*

MARY. How's your cock, Lord Gordon?

LORD GORDON. Bruised from the last encounter. Do I know you?

MARY. Mine's fighting fit. Will you pit yours against mine?

LORD GORDON. I never bet against a woman.

MARY. Afraid of bad luck? Scratch a parliamentarian, you find a follower of folk tales.

SOPHIE. Mr. Temptwell, it was him.

MRS. TEMPTWELL. So?

LORD GORDON. *(To Mary.)* When my cock recovers, perhaps.

MARY. Cocks recover so slowly and I presume you have no spare?

LORD GORDON. I have seen you before. *(Mr. Hardlong comes on. The men ignore him.)*

MARY. How can I remember a man who won't expose his cock? Are you looking for me, Mr. Hardlong?

MR. HARDLONG. No, for Sophie.

MARY. Who will fight my cock?

LORD EXRAKE. I have one.

MARY. At your age, Lord Exrake, it's still active?

LORD EXRAKE. My cock is young.

MARY. So, so, wondrous nature. Is it ready?

LORD EXRAKE. Spurred and trimmed. I've left your friend, she's charming but too quiet. At my age one needs a challenge, so I've come back to you.

MARY. I too need a challenge and I'd prefer to pit against Mr. Hardlong's cock. Will you?

MR. HARDLONG. I'll do anything if Sophie will stand by me.

MRS. TEMPTWELL. Sophie does what she's told.

MR. MANNERS. You ought to choose your opponents more carefully, Mary.

MARY. I didn't escape from propriety to fall into snobbery.

MR. MANNERS. That's a mistake. Snobbery is cheap to practice and has saved many a non-entity.

MARY. Just so. I don't need it. Where's my whip, Mrs. Temptwell?

MRS. TEMPTWELL. Don't bet too much.

MARY. Two hundred and fifty guineas, Mr. Hardlong? *(They touch their whips.)*

LORD EXRAKE. Ladies didn't have cocks in my day. *(They release the birds from the cloth sacs.)*

MARY. Now my bird, fight for me, match my courage and my strength. *(Screams and urgings from all.)*

MR. MANNERS. Your cock's dead.

MARY. No, look, look. It was a ruse. My cock's risen and stricken Mr. Hardlong's. Ha!

MR. HARDLONG. My cock's failed me.

MARY. That happens, Mr. Hardlong, even to the best. I keep winning I keep winning.

MR. HARDLONG. Will you come and console me, Sophie?

MARY. Mr. Hardlong, it is I who have the money. Will you come to me?

MR. HARDLONG. I want Sophie.

MARY. Does she want you? Sophie, come here. Here: Two hundred and fifty guineas. *(She throws her the sack of money.)*

SOPHIE. Oh, no, I can't.

MRS. TEMPTWELL. Take it.

SOPHIE. Thank you, Miss Mary.

MARY. Yes, but you must work for it. *(Pause.)* Nothing for nothing. That's their law. When they offer you money, you know what for. Well?

SOPHIE. I don't understand. *(Mary turns to Sophie and lifts up her skirts to her.)*

MARY. Men don't know their way around there. You will.

SOPHIE. I—

MARY. Look. Surely it's more appealing than their drooping displays? Or do you share their prejudice? *(Sophie kneels to Mary.)* What is it, gentlemen, you turn away, you feel disgust? Why don't you look and see what it's like. When you talk of sulphurous pits, deadly darkness, it's your own imagination you see. Look. It's solid, rich, gently shaped, fully coloured. The blood flows there on the way to the heart. It answers tenderness with tenderness, there is no gaping void here, only soft bumps, corners, cool convexities. Ah, Sophie, how sweet you are, I understand why they love you. Such peace. Shall we sleep? *(Two Old Women shuffle onto the stage, very very slowly.)* No — Look, over there, the spectres of passing time. I can't bear it. Wait. Mr. Manners, a race? You cannot question my choice of opponent. Four thousand pounds.

MRS. TEMPTWELL. That's all our money.

MR. HARDLONG. *(To Sophie.)* Let me take you away.

MR. MANNERS. Set it up, Hardlong. *(The two Old Women are placed side by side.)*

MR. HARDLONG. Gentlemen! Last chance to win your fortune in this unique event. *(He takes the bets.)* Mr. Manners' hag is favorite. *(All get ready. Lord Gordon raises his arm. The two Old Women stand.)* Go! *(The two Old Women start to run as fast as they can, which is extremely slowly. They cough, spit, stumble, pant, covering just a few feet.)*

MRS. TEMPTWELL. Four thousand pounds. We'll go hungry if she loses.

SOPHIE. We've been well fed.

MR. MANNERS. Faster, faster. There's a good girl.

LORD EXRAKE. I've put money on Miss Mary's hag, her ankles look firm.

LORD GORDON. Mr. Manners' hag is taking the lead, Miss Mary's hag having a little trouble.

MARY. A cane to your back if you stumble again. Pick you feet up!

MR. MANNERS. Come on, girl, you can do it.

LORD GORDON. Miss Mary's hag catching up. Is she? Yes she is. No, she's just tripped.

MARY. Your hag tripped mine, Mr. Manners. I saw.

LORD GORDON. No, there was no foul play. Mr. Manners' hag still in the lead, and gaining.

LORD EXRAKE. Get up, girl, get up. Go.

MR. HARDLONG. She's too broad in the back, bad for balance.

MR. MANNERS. Faster, faster.

LORD GORDON. Miss Mary's hag a little winded. Making an effort, yes, she's closing the gap. Yes. Will she do it?

MR. MANNERS. Steady, girl, steady.

LORD GORDON. Miss Mary's hag pulling ahead, yes, Mr. Manners' hag slowing down.

MARY. Go on, you can do it.

SOPHIE. She's ahead, she'll win. Faster. Faster.

MRS. TEMPTWELL. You're cheering yourself on. That could be us.

SOPHIE. You cheer her on.

LORD GORDON. Miss Mary's hag now well in the lead. Yes. Mr. Manners' hag stumbles. *(They cheer.)*

LORD EXRAKE. I've always been a good judge of ankles.

LORD GORDON. Only a few steps to the finishing line. It looks like Miss Mary's hag will win. But no. Look. Oh, what a jump. Look at that, what an effort and is it? Yes it is. It's Mr. Manners' hag first, what a superb effort, what a close race, but it's Mr. Manners' hag. *(More cheers.)*

MARY. I saw him give her brandy.

MR. MANNERS. That is not against the rules.

LORD GORDON. Mr. Manners never breaks the rules. You owe him four thousand pounds.

MRS. TEMPTWELL. Don't give it to him. He likes you. Burst into tears.

MARY. What? Turn female now?

MRS. TEMPTWELL. *(To Sophie.)* We go hungry for her vanity.

MARY. Here, Mr. Manners. I've lost.

MR. MANNERS. I have that effect on people.

LORD EXRAKE. I once lost two thousand pounds on a woodlice race. No one wants to know you when you've lost, but they forget. A few weeks in Ipswich always helps.

MR. MANNERS. Where's my hag? Here's a shilling for you, you ran well. *(The other Old Woman approaches Mary who ignores her.)*

OLD WOMAN. Please, Miss.

MARY. Let's go.

OLD WOMAN. I ran for you.

MARY. And lost. Don't touch me.

OLD WOMAN. I've been ill. Be kind.

MARY. Why? Look around. Do you see kindness anywhere? Where is it?

OLD WOMAN. Give me something.

MARY. I'll give you something priceless. Have you heard of knowledge? *(She takes the whip and beats her.)* There is no kindness. The world is a dry place.

OLD WOMAN. Please.

MARY. What, you want more? *(She beats her again. The Old Woman falls.)* Have I hurt you? *(She bends over her.)* I've seen her before. Or was it her sister? Why do you all stare at me? She was standing outside church. My father told me to give her some money. He gave me a coin. I gave her the coin, smiling. She smiled. I smiled more kindly. My father smiled. I followed his glance and saw a lady and a young man, her son. They were smiling. My father gave me another coin. I moved closer to her, my steps lit by everyone's smiles. I remember watching the movement of my wrist as I put the coin in her hand. I smiled at its grace. *(Pause.)* Was that better? Tell me, was that better?

INTERVAL

38

ACT THREE
Scene 1:

*Vauxhall Gardens at night. Mary and Mrs Temptwell stand in
the dark, waiting. Music and lights in the background. Mary
has a rounded stomach under dirty clothes.*

MRS. TEMPTWELL. Voices. Coming this way. *(They listen.)*
MARY. They've turned down another path.
MRS. TEMPTWELL. They're coming closer.
MARY. They've turned away. Your hearing's blunt. *(They
listen.)*
MRS. TEMPTWELL. Footsteps on the grass.
MARY. *(Listens.)* They're not his.
MRS. TEMPTWELL. You can't know that. Shht.
MARY. Those footsteps bounded my happiness for eighteen
years. I'd recognise them now. Damn. This itch. *(She scratches her-
self. Listens.)* Shht. No.
MRS. TEMPTWELL. Are you miserable?
MARY. You're waiting for my yes, aren't you? You'll chew on that
yes like a hungry dog, spit it up and chew again. Well, you can beg
for your yes. Do a trick for me, Mrs. Temptwell. Say something
interesting. You know I hate silence. And stop smiling.
MRS. TEMPTWELL. You're seeing things.
MARY. I saw your evil grin through the darkness. Cover up your
teeth, please, they make me ill.
MRS. TEMPTWELL. It's your condition. I told you to sit.
MARY. Damn this leech in my stomach, sucking at my blood,
determined to wriggle itself into life. Why can't you do something
about it. you old wizzard?
MRS. TEMPTWELL. If I was the devil we wouldn't be shiver-
ing in Vauxhall gardens waiting for our supper.
MARY. I could kill the man who did this. I found him in the
Haymarket, he looked strong, seemed to have some wit and the
night was soft and thick. We went to Westminster Bridge. I liked

that, the water rushing beneath me, cool air through my legs, until I discovered he was wearing a pigskin. New invention from Holland, he explained. He wouldn't catch my itching boils and I'd be protected from this. Fair exchange. So I had this piece of bookbinding scratching inside me and his words scratching at my intelligence, I'd mistaken talkativeness for wit. I hope he caught my infection. Footsteps. No. Why is it the one time I had no pleasure my body decided to give life? What's the meaning of that? Why don't you answer? Why do you never say anything? Has it ever happened to you? Were you ever young? Answer my questions, damn you. Who are you?

MRS. TEMPTWELL. It won't interest you.

MARY. You don't know what interests me.

MRS. TEMPTWELL. If you had an interest in anybody else, you wouldn't have thrown all your money away.

MARY. I was only trying to determine whether greed was the dominant worm in the human heart. I admit the experiments were costly. You didn't have to stay.

MRS. TEMPTWELL. I hear something.

MARY. Let's rob the first person who comes.

MRS. TEMPTWELL. Don't you want to see him? Find out how deeply he's mourning his dear dead daughter?

MARY. How easily he cancelled my existence.

MRS. TEMPTWELL. He's in the Cabinet now. He's happy.

MARY. Tell me a story.

MRS. TEMPTWELL. I don't know any.

MARY. Go away then. Do you enjoy this misery? Distract me, damn you. Tell your story. Where were you born? Don't you dare not answer.

MRS. TEMPTWELL. The country.

MARY. The country. The country. There are trees here.

MRS. TEMPTWELL. The North.

MARY. I know that from your granite face. Where?

MRS. TEMPTWELL. Don't shout or they 'll hear us.

MARY. Then talk. Remember something.

MRS. TEMPTWELL. I had a grandmother.

MARY. I had a father.

MRS. TEMPTWELL. She was hanged as a witch.

MARY. That's better.

MRS. TEMPTWELL. That's all.

MARY. Aren't there laws against hanging witches?

MRS. TEMPTWELL. It depends on the magistrate.

MARY. And she taught you to cast spells?

MRS. TEMPTWELL. She was an old woman, and poor. She talked to herself because she was angry and no one listened.

MARY. Tell me more. Tell me everything.

MRS. TEMPTWELL. They put a nail through her tongue.

MARY. And then?

MRS. TEMPTWELL. She was naked. I remember how thin she was. And the hair, the hair between her legs. It was white. That's all I remember.

MARY. Did people cry?

MRS. TEMPTWELL. They laughed. I laughed too once I'd forgotten she was my grandmother. The magistrate laughed loudest. She'd been on his land and he'd taken her cottage but she stayed at his gates, wouldn't leave. She asked for justise, he heard a witch's spell.

MARY. How interesting to have so much power and still so much fear.

MRS. TEMPTWELL. He also enjoyed humiliating her. Everyone did. It's an unusual experience...

MARY. Tell me, Mts. Temptwell, are we imitators by nature wishing to do what we see and hear. Or is every crime already in the human heart, dorment, waiting only to be tickled out?

MRS. TEMPTWELL. Footsteps.

MARY. His. *(Giles and Sophie appear. She is leading him.)*

GILES. Where are you taking me, my sweet? No need to come this far.

SOPHIE. I'm afraid of being seen, Sir.

GILES. Let's stop at this tree.

SOPHIE. This way, Sir.

GILES. I'm in such a hurry.

41

MARY. Here, Sir.

GILES. Who's that?

MRS. TEMPTWELL. A woman, Sir.

GILES. Sophie, where are you?

MRS. TEMPTWELL. Forget Sophie, Sir, she's docile but dull. Look here.

GILES. I can't see anything.

MARY. Here, Sir, I'll entertain you.

MRS. TEMPTWELL. She's fanciful and clever and I'm practical and knowing, if not so young.

GILES. I want a woman, not a personality. Sophie...

MRS. TEMPTWELL. A drawbridge; the treasures are here.

MARY. Here, Sir.

MRS. TEMPTWELL. Go to Mary.

GILES. Mary...

MRS. TEMPTWELL. Lovely name, Mary, isn't it?

GILES. Sophie's young. I want someone very young.

MARY. I'm young, Sir and know things Sophie does not know. Don't turn away, Sir, rejection is so painful. Come here.

GILES. If it means that much to you ... this isn't a trick? You're not more expensive?

MRS. TEMPTWELL. Labour is cheap, there's too much of it. And it's not as good as the machines. Perhaps one day this too will be done by machines. Would you like that, Sir?

GILES. At least machines don't talk.

MARY. But my conversation, Sir, is my greatest charm. Come.

GILES. It's so dark.

MARY. Isn't light the greatest mistake of this century? We light the streets only to stare at dirt. As for the lantern we poke into nature's crevasses, what has it revealed? Beauty? Or the most terrifying chaos? And if I take a close look at nature now, I mean, your nature, what will I find? *(As she talks, she unbuttons Giles.)* That it's tame, Sir, most tame, but our gardeners have taught us to make it wild, with the help of a little art.

GILES. *(Feebly.)* Must you talk so much?

MARY. It's my father who taught me to talk, Sir. He didn't suspect he'd also be teaching me to think. He was not a sensitive man and didn't know how words crawl into the mind and bore holes that will never again be filled. What is a question, Sir, but a thought that itches? Some are mild, the merest rash but some are cankerous, infectious, without cure. Do you have children, Sir, to grace your old age? Men often tell me I remind them of their daughters. You look sad, Sir, is your daughter dead? Did she die of a chill? That happens with women of graceful breeding, the blood becomes too polite to flow through the body. As long as she died young, men prefer that. I've heard many confessions. One man told me he locked up his wife for seventeen years and she still had the vulgarity not to die. Age, after all, is a manly quality. But even manly age, it seems, needs a little help if we're to get anywhere. A rub, will that do? *(She begins to massage him.)* It helps men to think of their daughters when I do this. You didn't kill yours, did you? Ah, I see it works. We're ready. Front or back? Oh, the bird's already flown the cage. Happens. Must have been the thrill of my conversation. Or thinking of your daughter. *(Mary uncovers her face.)* But you recognised your daughter some time ago, Papa, by the grace of her conversation. *(Pause.)* How did you say your daughter died? Did you starve her with your puny rations of approval? Immolate her to the country's future? But she's here. Look.

GILES. I have no daughter.

MARY. My name is Mary Traverse. Your wife had little chance of fathering me elsewhere.

GILES. You're a whore.

MARY. Is a daughter not a daughter when she's a whore? Or can she not be your daughter? Which words are at war here: whore, daughter, my? I am a daughter, but not yours, I am your whore but not your daughter. You dismiss the 'my' with such ease, you make fatherhood an act of grace, an honour I must buy with my graces which you withdraw as soon as I disgrace you.

GILES. What do you want from me?

MARY. Two things. Look at me.

GILES. Tell me what you want.

MARY. I'm here, Papa. Here. Look at me. *(Pause. Giles looks.)* Good.

GILES. Why? I gave you everything.

MARY. Except experience.

GILES. You could have married a lord.

MARY. I said experience, not a pose. The world outside, all of it. This.

GILES. This! I did everything to keep you from this! I didn't live in a beautiful house like you as a child. I had to work hard. Very hard. Not just with my hands, I didn't mind that. But with people. I had to work at not being despised. I was able. I made money, started the potteries, bought land, made more money. Everything I make sells now. And I'm listened to. I wanted you to have the ease, the delights I never knew. I wanted to protect you from what I had experienced, the slights, the filth, protect you even from the knowledge I had experienced it.

MARY. It wasn't what I wanted.

GILES. Whenever I looked at you I could forget my first twenty years.

MARY. Yes, you took my future to rewrite your past. Oh father, don't you see that's worse than Saturn eating his own children?

GILES. I let you read too much, it's maddened you.

MARY. And when I try to explain you threaten me with a madhouse? How dare you!

GILES. I forbid you to speak to me in that manner!

MARY. You have no power over me, Papa. Your daughter's dead. Now for the second thing. I want money.

GILES. Here's fifteen guineas.

MARY. Money, Papa. Not its frayed edges.

GILES. It's the agreed price for a whore.

MARY. If I wanted to make money lying on my back, I would have married your lord, Papa.

GILES. But — you—

MARY. I learn. I do not whore.

GILES. I don't understand.

MARY. You don't try.

GILES. Why? But — if you — if you're not — we could forget — I'll find a way to bring you back. Some questions, it wouldn't matter. If you would come back ... as you were...

MARY. As your graceful daughter?

GILES. My beautiful and witty daughter.

MARY. Open your eyes. Look at me. *(Giles looks. Silence.)* Do you want me back? *(Silence.)* The father I want cannot be the father of 'your' daughter. And yet, I want a father. Could you not be 'my' father? Could you not try?

GILES. I'll send you a little money.

MARY. I see *(Pause.)* I want half your money.

GILES. No.

MARY. A small price to keep me dead, Papa. Your powerful friends are supping in these gardens. Shall I walk through the tables and cry you've whored your daughter? I'll be believed. I talk well. People love to think ill. Don't try to cheat me. I know how much you have, the factories, the shops, your share of the canal.

GILES. What's made you like this?

MARY. Experience is expensive and precise.

GILES. I can tell you one thing, Mary. At the end of all this, you'll find nothing. Nothing. I know. Goodbye. *(He leaves. Mrs. Temptwell steps out of the shadows.)*

MARY. The only time he says my name, it's to curse me. One more denial. And he can still make the world grow cold.

MRS. TEMPTWELL. Did you see the humiliation on his face? I loved it.

MARY. Why?

MRS. TEMPTWELL. He made his younger brother a magistrate. It was that magistrate who hanged my grandmother.

MARY. Ah.

MRS. TEMPTWELL. It's not something you need understand.

MARY. I no longer understand anything.

MRS. TEMPTWELL. At least you've experienced cruelty. Their cruelty.

MARY. Is that what it is?

MRS. TEMPTWELL. Didn't it give you pleasure?

MARY. No. Sadness. And then, nothing. The withering of the night. I'm cold.

45

Scene 2:

Vauxhall Gardens. Sophie by herself. Then Jack.

JACK. By yourself?
SOPHIE. Yes.
JACK. Always by yourself?
SOPHIE. Yes!
JACK. Want company?
SOPHIE. Yes.
JACK. No one to look after you.
SOPHIE. No.
JACK. Not here for the toffs!
SOPHIE. No!
JACK. I hate them.
SOPHIE. Yes?
JACK. Fat. We go hungry.
SOPHIE. Yes.
JACK. Hungry?
SOPHIE. Yes. *(He gives her some bread.)*
JACK. Here. Good?
SOPHIE. Yes.
JACK. Stole it.
SOPHIE. Yes?
JACK. Dangerous. But not wrong.
SOPHIE. No.
JACK. Ever seen them work?
SOPHIE. No.
JACK. Come here.
SOPHIE. Yes.
JACK. Jack.
SOPHIE. Jack. Yes. Jack. *(They kiss.)*

46

Scene 3:

Vauxhall Gardens. Mr. Manners, Lord Gordon.

MR. MANNERS. The mob can be good or the mob can be bad, Lord Gordon, it depends on whether they do what you want them to do.

LORD GORDON. I could lead them, I could lead anything if I were made into a leader. It's getting there I find difficult.

MR. MANNERS. Real power prefers to remain invisible.

LORD GORDON. I wouldn't mind not having the power. Just make me visible. Notorious.

MR. MANNERS. What can I do? I'm no more than a servant.

LORD GORDON. You, Mr. Manners? The man most feared in Parliament?

MR. MANNERS. A mere servant, I assure you. I serve, however, an awesome power.

LORD GORDON. The King.

MR. MANNERS. The King's only a human being, Gordon, a German one at that. No, I serve a divine power.

LORD GORDON. You don't mean God, you haven't become a methodist?

MR. MANNERS. Order, Gordon, order: the very manifestation of God in the Universe. Have you studied the planets?

LORD GORDON. Can't say I have, no. I look at 'em.

MR. MANNERS. Ordered movement, perfect, everything in its place, forever. That's why I like men who make machines. They understand eternal principles, as I do. As you must.

LORD GORDON. I'm good at adding.

MR. MANNERS. When you ride in your carriage, you mustn't sit back and loll in your own comfort, no, you must study and love the smooth functioning of the vehicle. And if a wheel falls off, you must take it as a personal affront. Do you understand?

LORD GORDON. Check the wheels of my carriage...

MR. MANNERS. So with the country. Our duty is to watch that no wheel falls off.

LORD GORDON. Do we wear splendid livery?

MR. MANNERS. What?

LORD GORDON. I would like to serve the country.

MR. MANNERS. Good.

LORD GORDON. When can I start?

MR. MANNERS. We must wait. The times are restless.

LORD GORDON. *(Triumphantly.)* The roads are bumpy!

MR. MANNERS. And dangerous.

LORD GORDON. Highwaymen lurking behind every tree!

MR. MANNERS. I think we've exhausted that, Gordon. It is clear we must find something new, and entertaining to the people.

LORD GORDON. Me!

MR. MANNERS. Who knows? Someone ... inevitably appears, usually thrown up by the mob itself. And then one must be vigilant ... persuasive...

LORD GORDON. Be good to have me. Keep them quiet.

MR. MANNERS. Who?

LORD GORDON. The families, you know, my uncle. The other old families.

MR. MANNERS. What do they say?

LORD GORDON. That they wouldn't invite you to their house. Have to invite me. I'm a relative.

MR. MANNERS. What else do they say?

LORD GORDON. Nothing much. Used to rule England, time to rule again, better at it, born to it, look at the mess, all that. I don't listen.

MR. MANNERS. In times such as these, Lord Gordon, many different people make claims for themselves. The good servant must look for what fits best into the order of things. It is not always obvious. It can even be surprising.

LORD GORDON. I'm here, Mr. Manners, as soon as you want a change.

MR. MANNERS. No, no, Gordon, you haven't understood:

whatever happens, nothing must change.

Scene 4:

Elegant lodgings. Mary and Sophie, well dressed, sit in silence.

MARY. I'm cold.

SOPHIE. Are you ill, Miss Mary?

MARY. In which part of the anatomy does sadness sit, do you know, Sophie? It's not in the heart because the heart's a machine. So tell me how in this perfectly ordered universe you explain the chaos of the human soul. My father's right. I'm too clever. The inside of my skin hurts.

SOPHIE. Here's Mrs. Temptwell with your milk. *(Mrs. Temptwell comes on.)*

MARY. Take it from her and tell her to go.

MRS. TEMPTWELL. Mary—

MARY. Make her go, Sophie.

MRS. TEMPTWELL. Mary—

SOPHIE. Mary wants you to go, Mrs. Temptwell. Go away. *(Mrs. Temptwell leaves. Silence.)*

MARY. How's your child?

SOPHIE. He died.

MARY. Did he? I didn't know. *(Pause.)* I'm sorry. *(Pause.)* Am I? Are you? *(Pause.)* You can have mine.

SOPHIE. Oh yes, Miss Mary, I'd like that. Please.

MARY. Why?

SOPHIE. Why what?

MARY. No. I don't want to know why. What's that noise?

SOPHIE. Shouting. The price of white bread has gone up again.

MARY. I thought you people ate brown bread.

49

SOPHIE. We don't like it. My teeth aren't strong enough to eat brown bread. The merchants are hiding sacks of flour to make the prices go up so the people have decided to find the sacks and take them by force. Then they'll buy the sacks at a fair price. Jack says it's happening all over the country. They've beaten some merchants.

MARY. Would you do that if you were hungry?

SOPHIE. Oh no.

MARY. If you were very hungry? I would. But I don't have to. Do you ever think about that?

SOPHIE. About what?

MARY. Come here. Closer. We're the same age. Why do you never look at me? *(Pause.)* Look into my eyes.

SOPHIE. They're very beautiful, Miss Mary.

MARY. What do you think of me?

SOPHIE. You're feverish, Miss Mary. I'll bring you a brandy.

MARY. I asked you a question. What do you think of me?

SOPHIE. I don't understand.

MARY. You have a mind. Tell me what it sees.

SOPHIE. The country, Miss Mary. Fields. The fields I used to walk in as a child. That's what it sees. Green.

MARY. What question does it ask?

SOPHIE. Questions? Yes. How can I be less tired? Why does my belly hurt? Is that what you call thinking? And how good white bread is. Sometimes I think about the baby, but not much.

MARY. What do you think about my life?

SOPHIE. I hope it will be a long one.

MARY. Are you pretending to be stupid?

SOPHIE. I don't understand, Miss Mary. *(Pause.)* I feel things.

MARY. What do you feel for me? Hatred? Contempt? Don't be afraid, Sophie, answer.

SOPHIE. I don't feel — that way. I feel the cold. And the heat even more than the cold.

MARY. Sophie!

SOPHIE. I don't have time to think the way you do. Please, Miss

50

Mary, let me get you some wine.

MARY. Do I disgust you?

SOPHIE. You found me on the streets. I had nothing.

MARY. I pushed you on the streets as well. You took my place with Lord Gordon. What did you feel then? What did you feel in the gambling den, servicing my pleasures? What did you feel?

SOPHIE. I don't know. I can't remember. Sometimes I don't feel I'm there. It could be someone else. And I'm walking in the fields. So I don't mind much. My brother used to touch me. He was strong and I learned to make it not me. I was somewhere else. But when I want to, with Jack, I'm there. And then not. It's not difficult.

MARY. I see. I'm not sorry then. Perhaps I never was. Tell Mrs. Temptwell to come to me with some ideas. *(Mrs. Temptwell come on immediately.)*

MRS. TEMPTWELL. I knew our quiet Sophie wouldn't entertain you long. You can go, Sophie.

MARY. No, let her stay. *(Pause.)* Well?

MRS. TEMPTWELL. I've seen some beautiful jewels we could acquire.

MARY. Jewels.

MRS. TEMPTWELL. There are women wrestling in Clerkenwell. You like that.

MARY. Do I? *(Silence.)* Will I have to kill myself to make the time pass? Something. Something. And I can't sleep. Do you have dreams, Sophie?

SOPHIE. I dream of a little cottage...

MARY. Oh stop.

MRS. TEMPTWELL. Why don't you go, Sophie?

SOPHIE. Jack dreams of a new world.

MARY. A new world? Does he? A new world ... who's Jack?

SOPHIE. He's — Jack. He's very handsome.

MARY. All men are handsome when we drape them with our longings. A new world ... even Sophie's Jack has more interesting thoughts than I do. Why?

MRS. TEMPTWELL. We'll think of something tomorrow.

MARY. Another endless round of puny, private vice? This isn't experience, Mrs. Temptwell, this is another bounded room. You promised more, remember? They must have more than this. What? Yes ... they go to war. They go to war...

MRS. TEMPTWELL. We could go to America.

MARY. Or they dream of new worlds. They let their imaginations roam freely over the future, yes, they think about the country, and then they rule the country. What sort of a new world does Jack dream of, Sophie. Who is Jack?

Scene 5:

A cobbler's basement in Southwark. Jack, then Mary, Sophie, Mrs. Temptwell.

JACK. A travelling preacher taught me how to read. I was sixteen. He wanted me to spread the word of God. But I didn't like the word of God. Fear and obedience. Obedience and fear. I heard another word. Freedom. The preacher said God would punish me for such devilish rebellion. And he did. I can't talk. I want to tell people about freedom. I can't explain it. I have other words: equality, justice, right, but they're rough stones that won't stand together to a make a house. I have a new world, in my head, I can't make it come out, I can't give it to anyone. I look across the river at those houses of tyrants, I know the world needs me, but I'm cursed. Silent.

MARY. I can talk, Jack, but until now I had nothing to say. I understand what it is to need freedom. I thought it was something only I wanted, but now I know it is a longing in every human heart. I have watched freedon, beautiful freedom, hunted from every street and I know what it is to bang at the doors of tyranny. I could speak for you, Jack, if you taught me what to say.

52

JACK. You?

MARY. Why not?

SOPHIE. She can help us, Jack.

JACK. You wouldn't understand about equality.

MARY. I know the humiliation of being denied equality, Jack, and that it is a dignity due to all, men and women, rich and poor.

JACK. There should be no poor. Government makes people poor. Do you understand about natural rights?

MARY. I used to talk about nature.

JACK. Everyone is born with them. Born.

MARY. Yes: Nature has given us certain unquestionable, inalienable, rights but these have been taken from us by those who set themselves above us.

JACK. We have to get them back.

MARY. Wrench back from an usurping, base and selfish government what is ours by right.

JACK. And the new world- the new world-

MARY. Will be a world ruled by us, for our delight, a world of hope for all. Oh Jack that's beautiful. Let's go tell everyone.

JACK. They tyrants: show them up.

MARY. We'll explain to the people that they worship an authority that mocks, abuses and eventually kills them.

JACK. That's it, Mary.

MARY. Let's go, let's go quickly.

MRS. TEMPTWELL. Where are you going?

MARY. There, where the power sits. Parliament.

MRS. TEMPTWELL. You're mad.

MARY. If you wish to talk like my father, go home.

MRS. TEMPTWELL. She only wants power, Jack.

SOPHIE. No, she wants our good.

MARY. In the new world, they will be identical. Let's go.

Scene 6:

In front of the Houses of Parliament. Jack and Mary try to get by the guard. A man in dark clothes comes on during the exchange, then two Old Women, then the Locksmith, then Giles.

JACK. Listen to her.

GUARD. I told you: no petticoats in the Houses of Parliament.

MARY. I'll unpetticoat myself if it's my underwear you object to. What I have to say is without frills.

JACK. We have the right to be heard.

GUARD. I know you: you're the one who keeps bringing petitions.

MARY. No petticoats, no petitions, what do you allow in that house which is supposed to represent us all?

JACK. Thieves and hangmen. Let the working man in.

MAN. *(To an Old Woman.)* Do you know that woman?

MARY. We'll change history if we go in there. Don't you want a change?

GUARD. No.

MARY. Wouldn't you like a world where everyone was free to choose their future?

GUARD. Not much.

MARY. Oh the precious maidenhood of a young man. No virgin shuts her legs as tight as you your mind. No new thought will ever penetrate to make you bleed.

GUARD. Watch your language, Miss.

MARY. What are they doing for you in there? What?

JACK. Nothing, that's what.

MAN. *(To the Old Woman.)* Has she ever spoken here before?

GUARD. And what would your world do for me, eh?

MARY. It would do what you asked because it would be a world you would have made. What have those in there done to deserve their power? Nothing.

JACK. They stole it from us, that's what.

MAN. *(To the Old Woman.)* You don't know her name, do you?

MARY. Our sons and daughters will share the land.

OLD WOMAN. I'm not giving anything to my daughter. She's a whore.

MARY. In the new world, there will be no whores, there won't have to be.

LOCKSMITH. If I want a whore and I can pay for her, I have a right to that whore.

MARY. No one has the right to pleasure at the cost of another's pain. In the new world, everyone will have their natural, just, share of pleasure. Think of a world where there is no hoarding of illbegotten riches, no more theft—

LOCKSMITH. What happens to the locksmiths?

MARY. A new world where there are no longer any families living in greed—

LOCKSMITH. I'm a locksmith. What good are locks without thieves?

MARY. You will make keys for all of us.

LOCKSMITH. Oh. No. You get paid more for locks than keys.

JACK. The working man pays for everything and gets nothing.

MARY. Do you know how much our King costs us?

MAN. This is sedition.

MARY. Eight hundred thousand stirling a year.

MAN. *(To the Old Woman.)* Remember what she says, will you. *(The Man leaves quickly.)*

MARY. How much bread does eight hundred thousand stirling a year buy?

OLD WOMAN. I saw the King the other day. He looks ever such a gentleman.

LOCKSMITH. Why don't you go to America if you don't like it here? They make you pick cotton in the heat there and you die in two weeks.

MARY. Who was the first King of England? A French bandit.

OLD WOMAN. I didn't know that. Is that why he speaks so dif-

55

ferent from us?

JACK. A King's privilege is an insult to the working people.

MARY. What does the King do for us?

LOCKSMITH. If that was my daughter, I'd have her locked up.

GILES. Why? She speaks well. What she says is wrong, of course.

MARY. Let us share in the building of a new world.

JACK. All men will be brothers.

MARY. A world that is gentle, wise, free, uncircumscribed.

GILES. I used to have dreams like that.

MARY. Imagine how you would run this world and now, ask yourselves this: why have we no bread to eat?

OLD WOMAN. I've asked that before. No one tells me.

MARY. Ask yourselves why our children are born to hunger and toil.

OLD WOMAN. Why? *(Mr. Manners comes on from the Houses of Parliament.)*

MARY. Ask yourselves why they are indifferent to our needs.

OLD WOMAN/LOCKSMITH. Why?

MARY. Ask yourselves why they won't let us speak out.

ALL. Why?

MR. MANNERS. Why do you say all this here and not in there?

MARY/ALL. Yes. Why?

MR. MANNERS. They'd like to have you in there. They are interested in what you have to say.

JACK. They don't let the people in there.

MR. MANNERS. That can change.

MARY. You'll let us into the House?

MR. MANNERS. Not the House exactly, but there are many rooms.

MARY. Let's go.

MR. MANNERS. Just you — for the moment.

JACK. Go in, Mary. Talk to them about the people.

MARY. I'll see what they have to say and come back. *(Mary and*

Mr. Manners leave.)

GUARD. She was better out here.

GILES. People were listening to her. She made them listen.

JACK. She'll talk to them and come back.

GUARD. I've seen people go in there and come out very different.

JACK. Even they will have to listen to common sense.

GUARD. Are you going to this new world?

LOCKSMITH. I'm not having a world without locks.

Scene 7:

Preparations for a midnight conversation. Mrs. Temptwell and Sophie set out the chairs.

MRS. TEMPTWELL. We must stop her.

SOPHIE. Why? She's so gay.

MRS. TEMPTWELL. And us!

SOPHIE. She said I could go to the country and look after her child.

MRS. TEMPTWELL. No!

SOPHIE. Please don't stop me from having the child.

MRS. TEMPTWELL. She had you raped, she made you whore, she caused the misery that killed your child and now you'll slave to bring up her reject?

SOPHIE. She said we could have a cottage.

MRS. TEMPTWELL. Until she takes it away to make way for some roses. Don't you know what they're like?

SOPHIE. Who?

MRS. TEMPTWELL. Listen to these words. Sophie: freeborn Englishman. Aren't they sweet?

SOPHIE. I suppose so.

MRS. TEMPTWELL. My father was a freeborn Englishman. So

was yours.

SOPHIE. I never knew him.

MRS. TEMPTWELL. But us? I'm a servant. Nothing my own, no small piece of ground, no hour, no sleep she can't break with a bell. Do you understand, girl?

SOPHIE. Did you suffer misfortune?

MRS. TEMPTWELL. He was our misfortune, her father. I had to watch my mother grow thin as hunger and die. I curse the whole family.

SOPHIE. You could get another place.

MRS. TEMPTWELL. She'll be as low as us when I'm finished. And you could help, Sophie.

SOPHIE. I don't feel low.

MRS. TEMPTWELL. When you know all I know, you'll be angry too.

SOPHIE. When I've been angry, it's only made it all worse. No, I won't be angry. Is that all the chairs?

MRS. TEMPTWELL. We could work together. I'll be your friend.

SOPHIE. You said that when you brought me into the house.

MRS. TEMPTWELL. I didn't know how vicious she was. And now she'll do us even more harm with these ideas of hers.

SOPHIE. I like it when she speaks of the new world. So does Jack.

MRS. TEMPTWELL. New world? This is no way to get rid of the old.

Scene 8:

A Midnight Conversation: the last stages of a drunken dinner. Sophie, Mrs. Temptwell, Mary, Mr. Manners, Jack, the Guard, Lord Gordon.

MARY. Sophie, more wine for the gentlemen and for me.

MR. MANNERS. No more for me.

MARY. Moderation in all things, Mr. Manners?

MR. MANNERS. Historical moments need level heads.

MARY. Why? The future is intoxicating.

JACK. I'm a working man. I drink gin.

MRS. TEMPTWELL. And gin for me.

MARY. I forgot you, Mrs. Temptwell.

MRS. TEMPTWELL. That's what happens to working people, Jack.

GUARD. It's all going to change now.

MRS. TEMPTWELL. Is it?

MARY. I have asked you all here this evening that we may hammer out our common cause. Mr. Manners tells me it's a good time to be heard.

JACK. We want bread. Bread for everyone.

MARY. We have to ask for more than bread.

JACK. Every man has a right to eat.

MARY. It's a right remembered only by the hungry. No, we need something big enough to net the future.

JACK. All men are born equal.

MR. MANNERS. Too general. We don't listen to abstractions in England.

MARY. But we do need a good cry as our banner. I remember my father talking about the frenzy caused by the cry Wilkes and liberty.

LORD GORDON. What about Silks and Tyranny? *(Pause.)* Milk and bigotry? *(Silence.)* There's a Wilkes in the House. Tory chap isn't he?

MR. MANNERS. He's calmed down since the '60's. The House does that.

JACK. Liberty. We'd go for that.

MARY. Yes. Liberty is a beautiful word.

MR. MANNERS. Dangerous, Mary.

GUARD. Will there be liberty in the new world?

MARY. Oh yes. *(To Mr. Manners.)* Why dangerous? It's what we want.

MR. MANNERS. It's been heard before and no one understands it. People were shouting for Wilkes, not for liberty.

LORD GORDON. Gordon ... What about Gordon and Drollery? I do so wish to hear my name shouted.

MARY. Let us start again: to build a new world, one must know what is wrong with the old. What do you most want to be rid of, Jack?

JACK. Tyranny. I want to kill the tryants.

MR. MANNERS. That won't do, Mary.

MARY. Shouldn't we hear the people?

MR. MANNERS. One must interpret to lead.

LORD GORDON. You said I could be the leader in this, Mr. Manners, you said I could make myself know in History.

MR. MANNERS. You will, Lord Gordon.

LORD GORDON. I know: the French!

MARY. What about the French?

LORD GORDON. What I most want to be rid of. Hate them. Riot against them. No French!

MR. MANNERS. That's called war and we already have one.

MARY. Sophie, what do you most dislike?

SOPHIE. Me? I don't know. Bad smells.

JACK. That's my sweet lass.

LORD GORDON. Told you it was the French. No French Food. That'll rouse'em

MR. MANNERS. *(To Mary.)* There's actually a clue in all that.

MARY. Where? We're not getting anywhere.

MR. MANNERS. What makes a smell good or bad?

LORD GORDON. I don't know, but I know it when I smell it.

GUARD. What do smells have to do with the new world?

MRS. TEMPTWELL. There won't be a new world.

JACK. I don't understand any of this. I want to organize for bread and liberty.

MRS. TEMPTWELL. Go quickly before it's too late.

SOPHIE. No, Jack. Mary will help us. She's thinking for us.

60

MARY. Listen: Our lives ought by nature to be pleasant and free, but are not. Why? We have been invaded by unnatural practices and beliefs: the bad smells. What are they?

MR. MANNERS. Or: who are they?

MARY. Yes.

MR. MANNERS. The Dutch ... but one could hardly get emotional about the Dutch. The Jews ... not enough of them. The Irish...

JACK. I hate the Irish, they take lower wages.

MRS. TEMPTWELL. They work, like you. They're turning you against your own kind.

MARY. We must not turn against working people. What do all foreigners have in common?

LORD GORDON. They're not English.

MR. MANNERS. And not Church of England.

JACK. We hate the Church.

MARY. Yes. Anything that encourages superstition, hierarchy and prejudice is vile.

MR. MANNERS. That's not the Church of England. After all, the Church of England is more England than Church. The superstitions are unfortunate remains from former times ... when we were under the Catholics. Yes. The Catholics...

LORD GORDON. I'm to lead a mob of Catholics?

MR. MANNERS. You can't lead any mob, Gordon, you're in Parliament, remember? But you can present petitions...

MARY. We've done all that. We're wasting time.

MR. MANNERS. Did you know there's a bill about to be presented to the House which will give back to all Catholics their right to own property? There's already fear it will cause trouble. After all, the more the Catholics take, the less for people like Jack.

MARY. What do you think of Catholics, Jack?

JACK. I don't know much. They do smoky things on Sunday and come out smelling funny.

MR. MANNERS. It's much worse than that, isn't it, Mary?

MARY. Is it?

MR. MANNERS. Tell Jack about the Catholics. Tell him how

61

they stuff themselves with white bread on Sundays.

MARY. Ah, yes. They buy it all up and hoard it in their Chapels, that's why there's none left for you. Mr. Manners—

MR. MANNERS. Tell Jack about the Pope.

MARY. He is the tyrant of tyrants—

MR. MANNERS. The Pope has stores of bread in his palaces. He ships the bread secretly from England. He delights in eating Protestant bread. He would like to eat Protestants.

MARY. He makes them starve instead. Every day the number of hungry Protestants is read out to him and makes him laugh.

JACK. Where is this Pope? I'll kill him.

MARY. All Catholics are the Pope's slaves. If he tells them to drink the blood of Protestant children with their wine, they do.

MR. MANNERS. Protestant children have been know to disappear near Catholic chapels.

SOPHIE. Help!

MARY. It's the Catholics who've enclosed all the common land so they could build their chapels underground.

MRS. TEMPTWELL. Oh!

MR. MANNERS. That's right, Mary.

MARY. The Pope builds his palaces of luxury and depravity with the bones of murdered Protestants.

MR. MANNERS. Actually, the Pope is a woman. Her red robe is dyed anew every year in putrid blood.

LORD GORDON. That's disgusting.

MARY. The Pope washes his hands in the blood of tortured Protestant babes and drinks the tears of English mothers.

SOPHIE. Mothers against the Pope!

MR. MANNERS. That's not quite right.

MARY. Popery is the beast who claws at our freedom.

JACK. No to Popery, yes to Liberty.

MR. MANNERS. Excellent. I suggest we leave out liberty for the moment.

LORD GORDON. No Popery! Follow me.

MR. MANNERS. You, Lord Gordon, must present a petition to Parliament. It will be for the Repeal of the Catholic Relief Act.

LORD GORDON. How do you spell Relief?

MARY. You'll say the people don't want Catholics back in power. We'll explain all that later, but now we must rouse the people. Stop English babies from being roasted: No Popery!

SOPHIE. Save the children: No Hopery.

MARY. No. It's no Popery.

JACK. Save the working man: No Popery!

GUARD. This new world...

MARY. Later, later. No poverty: No Popery!

MRS. TEMPTWELL. No fences: No Popery!

ALL. No Popery. *(The knock over the chairs. They chant.)* NO POPERY. NO POPERY. NO POPERY.

Scene 9:

The Streets of London. Mary, Mr. Manners, Lord Gordon.

MARY. There are at least sixty thousand.

MR. MANNERS. Assembling in Lambeth.

MARY. A headless snake winding its way towards Westminster Bridge. I'm breathless.

LORD GORDON. I'm a little nervous too.

MARY. It's a time for you to go, Lord Gordon.

MR. MANNERS. Do you have the petition ready?

LORD GORDON. Here. In my hand. Both hands.

MR. MANNERS. Present it at half past two. Parliament is certain to delay any consideration of such a petition. Announce this to the crowd.

MARY. Tell them Parliament is on the side of the Catholics.

LORD GORDON. There are so many, I won't be hurt, will I?

MARY. Hurry, Lord Gordon, they're moving fast.

LORD GORDON. I never liked crowds.

MARY. Once they've surrounded Parliament, you won't get through.

LORD GORDON. It's not an easy thing to become a historical figure. *(He leaves.)*

MARY. Thousands and I've roused them. Oh, this is a delight beyond anything. Aren't you enjoying yourself?

MR. MANNERS. No. I like quiet. I'll be happy when it's over.

MARY. But this is a beginning. A new surge, which I shall lead.

MR. MANNERS. To what?

MARY. Freedom.

MR. MANNERS. You could be very useful, Mary, but you have a lot to learn. Power, however, is a brilliant master. Ah, listen. shouts. The crowd's beginning to be unruly. It usually takes an hour or two, a few well-placed rumours ... *(Sophie and Jack run on.)*

SOPHIE. Parliament won't save us from the Catholics.

JACK. We'll save ourselves from the Catholics.

SOPHIE. We went to Duke Street.

JACK. Where there are many Catholics.

SOPHIE. We found the Chapel of the ambassador from Gardenia.

MARY. Gardenia?

SOPHIE. It's a Poperist island, they capture ships and make shoes from the bones of sailors. They speak horrible spells in ill-latin.

MARY. Sardinia!

JACK. No Popery and wooden shoes! We burnt the Chapel.

SOPHIE. No Popery!

JACK. We're looking for the Bavarian Chapel.

SOPHIE. Burn it! No Popery!

BOTH No Popery! *(They go off.)*

MARY. Let's go. Let's go and lead them.

MR. MANNERS. Power always moves from behind. Let the bodies move forward.

MARY. I'm drunk with what I've done: glory! *(The Guard runs on. Increasing noise of riot in the background.)*

GUARD. We're thousands but act like one. We have the strength to build the new world. Yes, we'll have all we want, we'll share it, we're one.

MARY. Yes, yes. And it's by my command. I've done it all. *(Jack and Sophie come on.)*

JACK. The Bavarian embassy: burnt. On to Wapping. Find the Catholic houses and throw all the content onto the street. Burn, burn it all. There's a house belongs to a Protestant manufacturer, we're going to leave it, but someone shouts: why? Catholic or not, why should anyone be possessed of more than a thousand a year. Yes. Why? Burn it to the ground.

SOPHIE. No Popery. Freedom for all. Set the Protestant prisoners free. To Newgate!

JACK. To Bridewell!

BOTH. No Popery. To Clerkenwell! *(They rush off.)*

MARY. This burning makes me a little uneasy, Mr. Manners.

MR. MANNERS. If you want to chop wood, you must expect the chips to fly. Are you afraid?

MARY. No indeed.

MR. MANNERS. It has never been possible to define freedom.

MARY. What?

MR. MANNERS. Nothing. It's getting dark. Shapes lose their firmness. *(Jack comes on, followed by Sophie. Noise and fire in the background.)*

SOPHIE. Lord Gordon has presented the petition five times and Parliament has refused to consider it five times. And now they want to go home and sleep. We're rough handling the ones we catch. they're afraid to come out.

JACK. We're collecting for the poor mob. Give to the poor mob. For the poor mob.

SOPHIE. Here. Here's a penny for the poor mob. But I am the poor mob. *(The Guard runs on.)*

GUARD. No Popery and wooden shoes. To Holborn!

JACK. To Holborn!

SOPHIE. To Holborn! *(They run off.)*

MARY. Why Holborn?

MR. MANNERS. Streets and streets of distilleries. And they all belong to Catholics — or so the rumour goes.

MARY. I don't understand. I feel so powerful I can't think anymore. Look. Fire.

MR. MANNERS. There are twenty thousand gallons of gin in Holborn.

MARY. Oh God!

MR. MANNERS. God? *(Silence. Mrs. Temptwell comes on slowly, charred. She speaks coldly and quietly to Mary.)*

MRS. TEMPTWELL. It was dark, only a few thousand of us left. Prisoners, enthusiasts, those who couldn't free themselves from the throe of the crowd. We heard "to Holborn." We moved, step by step, pushed, pushing. Torches were at the front. We heard there was gin inside the houses, gin to refresh the poor mob. We rushed in, we fell in, pressed against the houses, torches high. I was pushed, I dropped, on my knees, drank the liquid, warm, then burning, looked up to see all coated in flames, fire rippling along the gin, houses, people clothes, all burning. *(Pause.)* Bodies pushed each other into the burning river, slid, still trying to drink, lapped at the fire. Women, children, tearing off their clothes. People laughed. Laughed. A man next to me found a girl, rolled her into the fire, pulled up her skirts. A wall crumbled over them.

MARY. Stop.

MRS. TEMPTWELL. Arms, arms, waved underneath bodies. Faces, shouting, mouths black, teeth chattering: dogs snapping at the edge of hell. A woman grabbed me. "I was just looking," she said, "why me?" Her cindered scalp peeled off.

MARY. Stop it!

MRS. TEMPTWELL. The smell. It was the smell. I fainted, slept. All quiet, the fire onto other houses. Moved a leg, shoved a body off me, crawled on cushion of corpses, soft, nothing much left.

MARY. It's not true. It didn't happen. *(Mrs. Temptwell opens a bundle she's been carrying, ashes and bones, and throws them over Mary.)*

MRS. TEMPTWELL. Look carefully through the teeth and you'll find some gold.

MARY. No! No! It cannot have happened. *(Jack runs on, his clothes are smouldering.)*

JACK. Water. I'm burning. Gin. The working man's in flames. Help me. *(Sophie rushes to him.)*

SOPHIE. Jack! Jack! *(She laughs, drunk.)* We've burnt everything. No Popery. No nothing. Jack. Damn them. Damn everything. Jack! *(She punches him, laughing. They fall over and roll off, together.)*

MARY. Oh my sweet Sophie. No. *(The Guard comes on.)*

GUARD. Where's my new world, where is it? Where? *(He leaves. Giles Traverse comes on.)*

GILES. They're moving towards the Bank of England, Mr. Manners.

MR. MANNERS. Ah. That must be stopped.

GILES. *(To Mary.)* So you've been involved in this horror?

MARY. I didn't want it to be like this. Please believe me. I wanted something good. I had dreams.

GILES. I heard them. I could have told you how quickly private dreams become public nightmares.

MARY. Why didn't you warn me?

GILES. Would you have listened?

MARY. Help me.

GILES. How can I, Mary? You're accountable now.

MR. MANNERS. Tell them to send the soldiers, Giles. And for the soldiers to shoot.

MARY. No!

GILES. You can't do that, Mr. Manners.

MR. MANNERS. If you don't agree with our policies, Giles, you need not stay with us.

GILES. This isn't policy, this is crime.

MR. MANNERS. Do what I ask or you will be suspected of condoning this horror and encouraging these criminals

MARY. This isn't what I wanted!

67

GILES. Do we ever know what we want? *(He leaves.)*

MARY. Don't let them shoot, don't.

MR. MANNERS. There is nothing so cleansing as massive death, Mary. People return with relief to their private little pains and stop barking at the future. It's what they want. This will last forty years at least, forty years of rule and order.

MARY. Damn your order and your rules.

MR. MANNERS. Don't damn the rules, Mary. Rules keep you from horror and emptiness. They bring peace to the heart, they're clear and simple, they hide the lengthening shadows. I'll do anything to keep the rules safe, not only for myself, but for the good of the world. One day all men will understand the beauty of rules. *(Lord Gordon rushes on.)*

LORD GORDON. They say it's my fault. They want to arrest me. Save me.

MR. MANNERS. We will. Give us time. Go to them now.

LORD GORDON. *(To Mary.)* I've just remembered where I saw you. I didn't mean to, that is, I didn't know-it didn't seem to matter. They're coming for me. It was better to be nobody. *(Lord Gordon runs off. The shooting starts.)*

MARY. Please, please tell me it isn't so. *(She screams. The shooting continues.)*

MRS. TEMPTWELL. *(Who has been piling the bones into a neat little pile.)* One, two, twelve, one hundred, two hundred and forty thousand, three million, six million, twenty million, thirty eight, two, eighteen, one, four, one.

MARY. Please tell me it did not happen.

ACT FOUR
Scene 1:

Lodgings on Oxford Street, near Tyburn. Sophie has a baby in her arms. Mrs. Temptwell tries to get near her.

SOPHIE. I love her.

MRS. TEMPTWELL. That's a title to nothing. Give her to me.

SOPHIE. I've looked after her well.

MRS. TEMPTWELL. You always were a fool.

SOPHIE. I want to see Miss Mary.

MRS. TEMPTWELL. Do as you're told. *(Mary comes on. She's half-dressed, a mess. She drags herself to a chair and collapses.)*

MARY. Find a shoe for my right foot, Mrs. Temptwell.

MRS. TEMPTWELL. I don't know where they are. *(Mary kicks off her one shoe.)*

MARY. There. Order. No. *(She stares vacantly at one of her legs, then rolls down her one stocking. She stops.)* Leave it. *(To Sophie.)* What are you doing here?

SOPHIE. You wanted to see your child?

MARY. Did I?

MRS. TEMPTWELL. The future citizen of the new world.

MARY. Stop. Yes: The last act.

SOPHIE. Let me take her back to the country. We're very happy. Jack is coming soon.

MARY. Jack.

SOPHIE. They'll let him go soon, he didn't do anything.

MRS. TEMPTWELL. You don't have to do anything to get yourself killed. Give us the child.

SOPHIE. Why?

MARY. Don't use that fateful word. Has that woman tempted you as well? Run.

MRS. TEMPTWELL. You did what you wanted.

MARY. Did I? I wanted knowledge, but I didn't know what it was. Even God wouldn't love this world if he existed, and I know he doesn't because Voltaire said so and Voltaire is a wit and the truth can only be funny. *(To Sophie.)* You never laugh.

SOPHIE. What will you do with her?

MARY. Look at us — crumbling. Too charred to scavenge for more hope. Soon we can stop breathing-last intake of the future. But it's not enough: our death won't redeem what's been. I am human. I know the world. I've shared its acts. And I would like to pour poison down the throat of this world, burn out its hideous memories. A white cloud to cancel it all. How? I don't know. But I can start here. I can look after what I've generated. Stop it.

SOPHIE. You want to poison your daughter.

MRS. TEMPTWELL. We're all poisoned anyway.

SOPHIE. You can't do that.

MARY. Is there anything of which we are not capable?

SOPHIE. You don't know.

MRS. TEMPTWELL. She knows everything.

SOPHIE. You're wrong. You don't know how to think, Mary. You think at a distance — too ahead or far back. If you just looked, from near.

MRS. TEMPTWELL. Our Sophie's found her tongue.

MARY. Just when I want silence.

MRS. TEMPTWELL. Must be that country air. Pink cheeks. pink thoughts.

SOPHIE. Stop, Mrs. temptwell, don't you dare. Listen to me, Mary. I know — about mornings.

MARY. The mornings?

SOPHIE. The first light of the morning. It's fresh, new. And I feel a kind of hunger in the mornings, but without the pain. Cold water on the skin. It makes her laugh too. Think about the mornings.

MRS. TEMPTWELL. Corpses look very fresh in the morning. You can go.

SOPHIE. In London too, the windows, the crisscross of the panes. You walk and then suddenly you're in one of the new squares, light. Don't you understand?

MRS. TEMPTWELL. We don't need an upstart bumkin preaching to us. Go.

SOPHIE. I will not. Miss Mary is unhappy about the world, but you, Mrs. Temptwell, are only full of hate. She hates you, Mary, she always did. *(Pause.)* She only wants to hurt you. Then she'll be happy.

MARY. Is that true? *(Pause.)* I suppose it's fair.

SOPHIE. No. It's wrong.

MARY. Not wrong, but small. As small as everything else. The world is made up of small particles of unspeakable ugliness. Why should I have the arrogance to claim a shared despair? *(To Mrs. Temptwell.)* Couldn't you have just strangled me in my cradle?

MRS. TEMPTWELL. I hate you, Mary, I hate your father, I hate your child, but she's wrong, it's no longer for what you did to me, no, it's for what you are. I know who you are, now, your kind. You're the evil spirits of this world, you keep us bound. Everything you touch goes wrong, but you always save yourselves and then go all poetic over other people's bodies. I know all we need is your death and then it won't go wrong again. Then there can be a new world. I'm starting here, but we'll get all of you.

MARY. More burning, more bones.

MRS. TEMPTWELL. The right bones this time. I'll laugh when I touch the ashes of thy kind, Mary Traverse.

MARY. I see. *(Pause.)* Perhaps you're right. But you could simply become addicted to counting bodies. And greed can attach itself to anyone. So. *(Pause.)* Let me have the child.

SOPHIE. You can't decide for anyone, Mary.

MARY. The child is mine.

SOPHIE. She's not yours. You gave her birth, that's all. Let her decide, when she's ready, when she knows.

MARY. Give her to me.

SOPHIE. She likes to watch the street.

MRS. TEMPTWELL. She'll see men on their way to be hanged at Tyburn. That's why we took these lodgings. It's the best attended amusement in London. *(Over this. Sophie has begun to sing an incredibly beautiful song. She moves away from both of them and goes on singing.)*

MARY. Listen.

MRS. TEMPTWELL. Shouts for death.

MARY. Listen to Sophie. Ha. A gracenote there. *(Sophie sings, watching the street.)* What are you looking at, Sophie, what is it you see?

SOPHIE. Look at the stone. The carved stone.

MARY. The new houses. Soft gray lines sloping against the London sky. *(Sophie sings.)* Do I have it all wrong? Sing Sophie. If I were God your song would appease me and I would forgive the history of the world.

SOPHIE. *(Giving Mary the child.)* Touch a baby's skin. It's the same thing.

MRS. TEMPTWELL. There's the cart. See who's in there, Sophie, and then sing to us.

SOPHIE. *(Screams.)* Jack!

Scene 2:

Tyburn. Sophie, Mrs. Temptwell and Mary, holding her baby. A Man pulls a cart. Jack is inside, alone. Lord Exrake follows the cart.

SOPHIE. Jack!

MARY. I tought it would be Lord Gordon.

SOPHIE. Jack!

MRS. TEMPTWELL. You don't like to hang lords.

SOPHIE. Jack. Speak to me. Jack. *(Jack is silent.)*

MAN. Let the cart pass.

LORD EXRAKE. Is he going to say something?

MARY. Lord Exrake!

LORD EXRAKE. Hello, my dear. Who are you? Forgive me ... my memory. What a sweet child. Not mine, I hope. No: too young. These days...

SOPHIE. Jack. It's me. Sophie. Speak to me. *(Jack is silent.)*

LORD EXRAKE. Sophie ... means wisdom. I have loved ... Did you ask why I'm here? I've found a way to go to sleep. I listen to what they say before they're hanged. I repeat their last words and it makes me sleep. Try it.

MARY. Is there no grace, somewhere?

LORD EXRAKE. *(To the Man.)* When will he talk?

MAN. Don't know. Some of them make jokes at the end. Some tell their lives, give speeches. I've never seen one who wouldn't talk.

LORD EXRAKE. Silence. Silence at the very end. Would that make me sleep?

SOPHIE. *(To Mary.)* You know he didn't do anything. Tell them!

MARY. Who will listen?

MRS. TEMPTWELL. Sing to her, Sophie.

MAN. *(To Jack.)* Look, I know how you feel. Animals out there aren't they? But you have a wife, right? Someone, anyway. Children? Well, there's a way you can take care of them when you're dead. Nothing magic. I work for this man: all you have to do is say this word we tell you and we'll look after your widow and any woman. What about it?

SOPHIE. Jack!

MAN. Look, she's cying for you. You don't want her to go hungry, do you? All you have to do is say, before the man — you know. Just before. All you say is: Drink Olvitie. Got it? Drink Olvitie. That's all.

LORD EXRAKE. That's what a man said a few weeks ago. Drink Olvitie. I've been drinking it ever since.

MAN. Remember that: drink Olvitie, and she'll be looked after.

SOPHIE. *(To Mary.)* You did all this. You should be up there. Go on. Kill your child. Here, I'll put it under the wheel for you.

MARY. Sophie, no. Not now. Not from you. I know we can ... we will find.

MRS. TEMPTWELL. You won't.

LORD EXRAKE. Have you lost something, my dear. Perhaps I can help you. What won't she find?

MRS. TEMPTWELL. Grace. She hasn't the right.

SOPHIE. Jack!

MARY. Come with me, Sophie. We will grieve, but we won't despair. Come. *(Mary takes Sophie in her arms and turns away her head. Jack stares, impassive. Silence.)*

LORD EXRAKE. Silence. Not even a curse.

(Schubert's Adagio in E flat major op, post 148 "Notturno.")

Scene 3:

A Garden in the Potteries. Mary, Sophie, Giles, Little Mary.

MARY. Beauty. Seen, unseen. I want to touch the light on the river. But we can't even see light. Perhaps one day we'll understand it.

GILES. Are you still trying to understand everything?

SOPHIE. When you told me the world was made up of little particles, Mary, I cried for days.

GILES. I was unhappy when I found out how old the world was.

MARY. I love your wrinkles, father.

GILES. Are there not things it is better not to know? Others it is best to forget?

SOPHIE. No. We must not forget.

MARY. And now the light lifts itself, streaks the chimneys. Gone.

GILES. Where's little Mary? I'll take her in. *(Mrs. Temptwell come on.)*

MRS. TEMPTWELL. This is my father's land. Try to throw me off.

GILES. No. That much I have learned. Other things too ... but I'm old. Speak to them.

MARY. I'm certain that when we understand it all, it'll be simpler, not more confusing. One day we'll know how to love this world.

MRS. TEMPTWELL. Will you know how to make it just?

GILES. Mary!

MARY. There she is.

BLACKOUT

75

PROPERTY LIST

ACT ONE

SCENE 1
Onstage
Chair

SCENE 2
Onstage
Carpet
Fan

SCENE 3
Offstage
Sword (Lord Gordon)

ACT TWO

SCENE 3
Offstage
Food (Sophie)

SCENE 4
Onstage
Cards (for piquet)
Birds (in cloth sacks)
Sack of money

Offstage
Whips (Mr. Hardlong and Mary)

ACT THREE

SCENE 2
Offstage
Bread (Jack)

SCENE 4
Offstage
Milk (Mrs. Temptwell)

SCENE 7
Onstage
Chairs

SCENE 9
Offstage
Petition (Lord Gordon)
Bundle of ashes and bones (Mrs. Temptwell)

ACT FOUR

SCENE 1
Onstage
Chair

SCENE 2
Offstage
Cart (Man)

A NOTE ON STAGING

It is crucial for each scene of this play to flow straight into the next. Props must therefore be kept to an absolute minimum and the set should serve the whole play. All of the action, with the exception of the very last scene, takes place in London and the set ought to be an abstract of London: the underneath of a bridge, a backdrop of houses, or a street. It should convey the beauty of the architecture of that period, as in the prints of Piranesi. The costumes should belong to the second half of the 18th Century, but again, they need not be naturalistic.

The first two scenes of Act One take place in Mary's house and can be played in front of the curtain if there is one, or a backdrop representing books. This is to accentuate the strangeness and darkness of the world that is revealed when Mary goes "outside" in the third scene.

The rape in Act One, scene 3 takes place offstage. It is Mary's reaction and description that matter.

The game of Piquet in Act Two, scene 4 is a real one and although the cards are necessarily blank, the actors ought to have a good understanding of the game.

The cock fight in Act Two, scene 4 and the "Midnight Conversation" in Act Three, scene 7 are illustrated in Hogarth prints and the staging should reflect those prints. Hogarth is in any case a very good guide to the world of the play.

The riot in Act Three, scene 8 takes place offstage and Mary and Mr. Manners remain very still throughout, as if watching it on television, but there must be a sense of the fire and the chaos approaching them.

In general, the most important thing is to keep the action as realistic as possible without looking for naturalism and without clogging it up with unnecessary furniture, decor, or gestures.

Act Four, scene 2, however, requires a real cart.

Timberlake Wertenbaker